The
Principles
of
Information
Ethics

The
Principles
of
Information
Ethics

Richard J. Severson

M.E. Sharpe
Armonk, New York
London, England

Library of Congress Cataloging-in-Publication Data

Severson, Richard James, 1955–
The principles of information ethics /
Richard Severson.
p. cm.
Includes bibliographical references and index.
ISBN 1-56324-957-X (hardcover : alk. paper). —
ISBN 1-56324-958-8 (pbk. : alk. paper)
1. Information technology—Moral and ethical aspects.
I. Title.
T58.5.S48 1997
174′.90904—dc21
96-52983
CIP

Printed in the United States of America

The paper used in this publication meets the minimum requirements of
American National Standard for Information Sciences—
Permanence of Paper for Printed Library Materials,
ANSI Z 39.48-1984.

∞

BM (c) 10 9 8 7 6 5 4 3 2 1
BM (p) 10 9 8 7 6 5 4 3 2 1

Contents

Preface

A generation ago, Americans suffered a moral crisis due to the automation of hospitals. For the first time in human experience, people who seemed dead (loss of heartbeat, loss of breath) could be revived by sophisticated drugs and machines.

Some patients snatched from death's jaws in high-tech hospitals go on living quality lives for many years; some become little more than machine-dependent vegetables. The latter possibility was the cause of our moral anguish. When is it appropriate to use every available means to save a life, and when is it appropriate to let nature take its course? That is a question we could not answer without the help of ethical reflection.

There is no question that technological advancements improve the lot of human existence. But new technologies also make life more complicated and confusing, as the case of hospital automation illustrates. My assumption in this book is that we have reached the same point of moral confusion and crisis with respect to information technologies that was reached a generation ago with respect to new hospital technologies.

Biomedical ethicists taught us how to rely on a short list of easily remembered principles when making tough decisions about life-and-death matters in the hospital setting. Likewise, I offer a list of four easily remembered principles that will help us make wise decisions when confronted with complex information age issues. For example, what would you do if the software company for which you work makes unrealistic promises to a potential new client? Or what kind of E-mail policy would you adopt in order to maintain a good working environment in the department that you manage? The principles discussed in this book—respect for intellectual property, respect for privacy, fair representation, and nonmaleficence—will help you answer these questions and many others like them.

This book has been written for students and interested general readers and is suitable as a textbook for classes in business, computer science, library science, information science, and ethics. As an ethics primer for people without a philosophical background, this book is grounded in common sense; every effort has been made to make it both readable and interesting. Many examples from movies, literature, business, and real life are incorporated into every chapter. Each chapter ends with questions for further thought that will encourage readers to think for themselves, and a number of case studies have been included in an appendix so that readers can practice the simple method of principled ethics introduced in chapter 1.

This book grew out of an ethics lecture I give in a required class at Marylhurst College in Portland, Oregon. Titled "Information Power," the class introduces students to a wide range of issues pertaining to postindustrial information society. Students are also taught the basic computer-mediated research skills that are necessary in these high-tech times.

I wish to thank the students at Marylhurst College for their lively interest in ethics and their thoughtfulness. As often happens in good classes, I have learned as much as I have taught. I also wish to thank Pierina Parise and Paul Gregorio for encouraging me to get involved in the Information Power class. Finally, I want to express warm thanks to Peter Coveney, executive editor at M.E. Sharpe, for inviting me to write this book and for supporting me from start to finish.

The
Principles
of
Information
Ethics

Chapter 1

Introduction to Principled Ethics

Almost thirty years before he published *The Origin of Species* (1859), Charles Darwin spent five years exploring South America's coasts as an unpaid naturalist aboard the ship HMS *Beagle*. The rigors of the trip—its isolation, physical labors, and abundant exposure to exotic species and geological formations—helped transform Darwin into a skilled observer and writer. At the southern tip of South America is the large island called Tierra del Fuego, which means "land of fire." It was heavily forested, cold, cloudy, and sparsely inhabited by tribal natives at the time of Darwin's visit. In his memoir, Darwin describes several encounters with the Fuegian people. He was struck by what interested (and did not interest) the Fuegians about their European visitors. They were fascinated by the colorful clothing of the Europeans and the rowboats that were used to shuttle from ship to shore. Darwin noticed that the rowboats were roughly the same size as the dugout canoes that the Fuegians used. But no Fuegians paid the slightest attention to the massive sailing ship that lay anchored in their waters. It was as if the ship were so far removed from the everyday world of Tierra del Fuego that the Fuegians had no way to conceive its purpose. Without conception of its place in their world, they were forced to pretend it did not exist.[1]

At first glance, it might seem appropriate to think of computer technology as a modern-day version of the *Beagle*. There is a temptation (at least for some of us) to "act like Fuegians" by avoiding computers and scoffing at people who hype the "information age." Taking a skeptical stance can be healthy and refreshing. In the end, however, we will all become efficient computer users. Automated teller machines (ATMs) are too convenient to ignore for long, as are automated library catalogs and even E-mail accounts. How the Internet works is not a worrisome question for generations raised on *Star Trek*. We know how to conceive exotic new technologies, which function more like Darwin's rowboat in our ever-changing society. Our difficulty is different from the Fuegians'.

We have become accustomed to an electronic world that is far removed from the rhythms of nature that used to govern human activities. When the sun goes down, electric lights give us other options than going to bed.[2] Telephones and television have created a sense of instant intimacy between cultures and places that used to be permanently foreign. CNN coverage of the nighttime bombing of Baghdad in 1991 comes to mind as an eerie example of how electronic media have overcome the age-old barrier of physical distance. As unregulated conduits of information and commerce, computer networks (the next evolutionary stage in electronic technologies) now threaten the integrity and meaning of national borders.

The benefits and blessings of life in the electronic age are undeniable. So, too, is the fact that we are becoming more and more dependent on technology. Technology dependence has made human life permanently more complicated. Complexity is one of the unthought consequences of life in an electronic world. It has infiltrated every aspect of our lives, including the way we think. Have you noticed this? There is a tendency to make everything more complicated. Now that we have the world of information at our fingertips on the Web, we don't know how to stop searching and come to a conclusion. Or think of the millions of new pages of law that are being promulgated by the federal government in order to maintain some sense of national "order." A New York attorney recently wrote a best-seller about how too much law is killing America.[3] He said that we have lost our common sense, and I agree. Whereas the Fuegians lived in a simple world and had difficulty conceiving complex intrusions, we live in a complex world and have difficulty grasping the simple truths that make life meaningful.

The ship that we have a tendency to ignore is not computer technology but our own moral compass. Morality gives direction to our lives because it enables us to determine what is good and what isn't. It is a deliberative practice that we acquire from our upbringing and culture. A critical part of our moral upbringing is the development of a conscience or inner voice that will guide us in our deliberations about what is good and right. Morality and conscience can't function properly, however, if we don't stop and listen. Here is the problem with too much technology dependence and complexity: we get so busy and fill our lives with so many distractions that we forget how important it is to sit quietly. Does it feel awkward when you find yourself alone in a silent room? If you are like me, your life is full and fast-paced: I usually read the paper with my breakfast, listen to the radio on the drive to work, log onto the computer first thing at my desk, listen to music on a portable CD player when I exercise, and watch television for relaxation at night. With so many opportunities to be entertained every moment when I am awake, there is little opportunity for reflection. Yet it is an essential part of human experience simply to ruminate about how and why to be good. How can I listen to my conscience if I don't make time for quiet reflection?

When we consistently ignore the moral reflection that gives meaning and direction to our lives, I believe there is an eventual negative effect. I agree with the *Time* magazine columnist who claims we may have created a world of false electronic intimacies that reduces our morality to a kind of sleaze entertainment whereby only the unimaginable (the horrible murder of Susan Smith's children, for example) gets through to us.[4] In other words, we have a tendency to become spectators rather than moral agents, easily bored, awaiting the next O.J. Simpson trial or billion-dollar Barings bank shutdown to break through the heavy flow of everyday news that anesthetizes us. When we forget to be our moral selves, we lose a sense of community or shared responsibility and start blaming others if life doesn't go exactly as we wish.

One hope I have for this book is that it will persuade you to take more time for moral reflection in our busy, technology-driven world. A moral compass is like muscle tone: it must be exercised frequently in order to maintain vigor. It is just as easy to forget about one's moral well-being as it is to forget about one's physical health. It may be hard to pinpoint the onset of difficulties due to the neglect of physical or moral exercise, but it isn't hard to see trends such as an increase in heart disease cases or civil lawsuits. The moral life requires nurture, especially in a time such as ours when it is easy to be distracted day after day. In the next section, I indicate how ethics can help us stay on track with our moral responsibilities. It is too late for the Fuegians to realize that the new culture represented by Darwin's visiting ship would eventually overwhelm their own culture; I hope we do not continue to ignore the increasingly invisible ship of our moral compass.

Morality and Ethics

Most people use the terms *morality* and *ethics* interchangeably. That is certainly acceptable, but I believe it leads to confusion about the purpose of ethics. As I have already suggested, morality refers to the sense of conscience and right and wrong that we derive from our upbringing. Morality is highly personal and often functions instinctively. Suppose I am shopping in a music store and the clerk leaves for several minutes. It would be tempting to pocket the CD I am inspecting and walk out the door. Let's assume there are no electromagnetic alarm systems to worry about, so the risk of being apprehended for shoplifting is very small. Then what happens? My conscience kicks in and tells me that stealing the CD would be wrong. Heeding my conscience, I decide to wait for the clerk to ring up my sale. This is a typical moral experience, which happens almost automatically (like a reflex). Ethics, on the other hand, is more structured and deliberative; it is a kind of critical thinking about the moral life.

In normal circumstances, our morality works fine. Its guidance and warning signals (the voice of conscience, a feeling of guilt or apprehension, an immediate conviction of being right or wrong) are usually enough to ensure our goodness. The problem is that our moral instincts don't function well in situations that are new and complex. As with most endeavors, like playing the piano, our morals depend on habit and practice. In order to become a good piano player, I must develop the habit of practicing every day; in order to become a good moral agent, I must also develop and practice good habits. What if I only practice chopsticks and simple melodies on the piano? No matter how much practice time I put in, I will be unable to play a Bach concerto because it would require experience and ability of a much higher order. This kind of discrepancy between levels of difficulty happens in the moral life, too. In order to overcome the gap between my piano experience and the experience required to play Bach, a guide or teacher must be found. The same is true for morality. Ethics is a guide for our morality when we face complicated situations that eclipse the level of our prior moral experience.

Ethics brings the discipline of thinking to the moral life so that we can figure out what to do when our instincts become overloaded. Think of what has happened in high-tech hospitals. New medical machines and drugs are capable of keeping people alive beyond the point of what we used to think of as natural death (i.e., loss of breath and heartbeat). The normal moral instinct to fight for life can become burdensome, even ludicrous, in some cases when life-sustaining technologies are misapplied. When do we stop using every available means to save a life and allow the patient to die with dignity? This is a dramatic example of how technological innovation can create a new and more complex world that outruns our moral experience. Over the past several decades, biomedical ethicists have developed a short list of ethical principles to which medical professionals can refer as they counsel patients and their families about options for treatment.[5] I believe that information technologies have advanced to the point at which an analogy to the hospital situation of a generation ago is appropriate.

One of the early symbols of moral crisis in health care was Karen Anne Quinlan's tragic story, which was widely reported in 1975 and 1976. Involved in a life-threatening accident at the age of twenty-one, Quinlan was in a deep coma and required the use of a respirator to breathe. Her parents asked that the respirator be turned off so that their daughter could die a natural death. The doctors refused because they believed it would violate their ethical obligation to protect life and avoid taking any action that might lead to a patient's death. A lower court upheld the doctors' position, but the New Jersey supreme court sided with the parents. Ironically, after the respirator was turned off, Quinlan began to breathe on her own and lived in a comatose state for more than nine years. This heart-wrenching case forced us to see that the ancient moral principle to do no harm (which had guided doctors for hundreds of years) was no longer sufficient in medical practice. Because of new and expensive technologies, other considerations are equally important. For instance, we must respect the privacy and autonomy of patients who wish to decline lifesaving measures. We also have to think about how much good is being done for the individual and society at large when great expense is incurred to satisfy a doctor's desire to preserve life. Biomedical ethicists try to point out the competing moral interests that are at stake in high-tech health care. Sticking to just one rule or principle (do no harm) is too simplistic now.

A number of cases are potentially just as important for information ethics as Quinlan's case was for biomedical ethics. There is the 1988 case of Robert Morris, the Cornell University student who devised a worm program that crippled much of the Internet, supposedly spreading as a virus to more than six thousand computers before being detected. Morris was suspended from school for violating the university's code of academic conduct. The punishment was little more than a slap on the wrist. Nevertheless, the case helped focus attention on the need for moral guidelines regarding computer networks. There is also the case of Colonel Oliver North's supposedly deleted E-mail regarding the illegal sale of arms to Iran and the subsequent transmission of aid to the contras in Nicaragua. An operative in the Ronald Reagan administration, North sent E-mail messages to Admiral John Poindexter and others about his covert activities. North and Poindexter assumed that hitting the delete button erased all traces of their electronic correspondence. They were mistaken. Backup copies of North's E-mail were retrieved and used in court. The case focused attention on the proprietary issues surrounding electronic mail. Is E-mail the private property of the correspondents? Or does it belong to the employer that makes the system available?

Admiral Jeremy Boorda's surprising suicide in May 1996 seems especially analogous to the Quinlan case because it pertains to our perceptions of death and dying. There must have been many reasons for America's highest-ranking naval officer to end his life in such a fashion. One that he specifically revealed in two suicide notes pertained to the negative attention the press was paying to his Vietnam medals. The media were questioning his right to wear combat "v" insignia. To blame the media for Boorda's death would be unjust. But we must wonder about the "in-your-face, rush-to-judgment" mentality that often prevails in our society. News is not just the news anymore; it has to compete with other entertainment venues. In an information society, the average story cannot break through the glut of competing stories without being sensationalized to some extent. When a child starves in an African village, the whole world can witness it through television. This capacity to publicly document every event and experience often creates situations of unbearable moral intensity, according to one ethical commentator.[6] I believe Boorda's sense of everyday morality was overrun by the unrealistic intensity and censure that is a consequence of high-tech media pressures. It is my contention that ethics, as disciplined reflection on the moral life, can help us to restore our sense of moral balance when life becomes overly intensified.

In a thoughtful tribute to Boorda, retired Admiral Leon Edney made the observation that Americans are losing the ability to debate and disagree.[7] In order to have a debate, we must first be civil. Civility is the public manifestation of our private morality. It requires that we be fair and charitable to those who disagree with us. That is precisely what we are missing. When someone makes a mistake, we pounce; when someone disagrees, we go for the throat. Why this incivility? There are many reasons. One of them is the problem of moral exclusiveness. Moral exclusiveness is the habit of believing that there is only one way to view something. Consider the abortion "debate" ("nondebate" would be more accurate). Prolife advocates shout across picket lines at prochoice advocates, and vice versa. In fact, the two sides seem to despise each other. There is little attempt to listen respectfully or seek common ground. That would be too risky, because another requirement of civility is goodwill. To be of good will means that we are willing to give ground when a better argument is presented. This is also something we are missing. Perhaps it is fear that keeps us so morally entrenched: we don't know what an acceptable alternative would be, so we hold onto our own position no matter what. We cherish the democratic entitlement to have and hold our own opinions, but we forget that democracy also requires us to enter into genuine dialogue and allow the better opinions to persuade us. Otherwise, there is no capacity for consensus, which is a necessity if democracy is going to work and not just atrophy into noncommunicative anarchy. We have developed the unfortunate habit of taking uncompromising moral positions. When we do that, it sends the message that no matter what anybody else says, we will not budge or change. This is moral exclusiveness, and it is destroying our civility.

More laws would make the problem of moral exclusiveness worse, not better. We need less external regulation and more internal regulation in order to recover our sense of fairness and goodwill. Our moral sensibilities need a booster shot in order to fight against the temptation to settle for easy, uncompromising answers to difficult problems. Ethics is that kind of booster shot; it can:

- Help guide and educate our moral instincts.
- Steer us away from uncompromising positions.
- Improve our moral vocabulary so that we might talk and listen better.

Ethics is in the service of morality. It cannot replace morality nor substitute for its absence. We turn to ethics for one reason only: so that we can make our morals slightly more capable.

Principles Are Not Rules

Moral reflection is a form of introspection, like meditation or listening. Given the busy world in which we live, it is necessary to make time for quiet listening. It gets us in touch with conscience and the heartfelt instincts we have about life and our own happiness. Moral reflection alone is not enough to prepare us for the complex problems of the information age, however. We also need the help of ethical reflection, which is less personal and more practical than moral reflection.

The practical problem that ethical reflection must solve is how to boost our morals so that we are better able to handle the new challenges that information technologies bring. There are many ethical theories and books that could help in this task of improving ordinary morality.[8] I think it is better, however, to keep the technical vocabulary and theory to a minimum. What we need is something straightforward and simple enough to incorporate into our own morality. Ethics must be in the service of morality; otherwise, it is just cheap talk. I am going to follow the example of the biomedical ethicists whom I mentioned previously and introduce you to a form of principled ethical reflection.

What is a principle? Before I introduce the four basic principles of information ethics, it would be helpful to reflect briefly upon the nature of principles. Principles are guidelines for our actions. They represent a summation of practical knowledge and experience. Like good advice, principles come to the point about what is crucial. They can usually be stated in one sentence or even one word. "Justice" is an example. This one word represents our collective commitment to treat people fairly. It is one of the most crucial aspects of our society, summarizing the wisdom of the American Constitution, which guarantees equal treatment and opportunity to all people. If, in my daily affairs, I normally test my decisions before I act on them to make sure that they honor my commitment to justice, then I am living a principled life. To live according to principle means that I keep in mind certain briefly stated guidelines that can influence my instincts and behavior for the better.

Principles summarize previous experience in an insightful way. Suppose you're one of those people who have trouble taking tests. You study hard, practically memorizing your notes, but then you don't perform well on the test. An adviser suggests that you practice a relaxation technique, which helps a little. Surprisingly, you get an A on a test for which you barely had time to prepare. Then it hits you that all this time you've been trying too hard. Instead of studying to the point of exhaustion and boredom, it is better to stay fresh and take frequent breaks. "Don't overprepare" becomes the principle by which you decide to live. It summarizes the hard lesson you learned about test taking.

Principles are flexible guidelines. That is one of the virtues of their brevity. "Don't overprepare" represents the wisdom of a hard lesson about taking tests, but it doesn't spell out a formula for precisely what to do in a given situation. In other words, principles are not rules. Rules entail more specific instructions about how and when to do something. If you tell your teenager, "I want you home by eleven o'clock," that is a rule. Telling your teenager to "use good judgment" about what time to come home would be the principled approach. Rules might be more appropriate in the case of a teenager's curfew. In ethical reflection, however, principles are more appropriate than rules.

To apply a principle such as "don't overprepare" to a specific situation (studying for next week's chemistry test), judgment is required. You must decide how much study time would be appropriate. In order to do so, you make a mental list of how much reading must be done, how many pages of notes reviewed, how much time devoted to other coursework, and so forth. Applying principles is a deliberative process; in the end, a creative and individualized judgment must be made about how the broad principle fits the particular circumstances. Applying rules, on the other hand, is nondeliberative. Part of the attraction of rules is that they suspend the need for judgment. If you have to be home by eleven, then you have to be home by eleven; there's nothing more to think about. Rules save us from having to think and make tough choices, but they also tend to make us inflexible and thoughtless. If, as I suggested earlier, we are becoming more uncompromising in our morals, it is probably because we have turned our moral principles into hardened rules. Perhaps it is an understandable mistake in a society such as ours, which is so given to finding legal solutions to every problem. Laws tend to be more like rules than principles.[9]

The hard moral lessons of the information age can be represented by four ethical principles, listed in Table 1.1. The purpose of this book is to help you appropriate the experience and wisdom that stand behind each of these principles. Making them part of your own moral experience will strengthen your abilities to resolve high-tech informational problems. Each of these principles will be the sole topic of a subsequent chapter. In addition, the appendix provides several case studies on which to practice the simple method of principled ethics introduced in the next section.

Simple Is as Simple Does

The movie *Forrest Gump* teaches the lesson that true simplicity is the same thing as profundity.[10] Forrest didn't al-

Table 1.1

The Principles of Information Ethics

1. Respect for intellectual property
2. Respect for privacy
3. Fair representation
4. Nonmaleficence (or "doing no harm")

ways understand the details about what was going on around him, but he usually responded appropriately because his actions flowed from a core sense of moral kindness. As much as anything else, it was fidelity to his mother's unusual principles ("Life is like a box of chocolates," "Stupid is as stupid does") that kept Forrest safe from the despair that afflicted Jenny and Lieutenant Dan. To paraphrase (somewhat) Mrs. Gump, I suggest that the answer to the complexities of the information age can be found in the statement "simple is as simple does." By that I mean two things. First, our moral simplicity (like Forrest's) must be nurtured and safeguarded by sticking to principles such as the ones discussed in this book. Second, our guiding principles must be grounded in the activities of real life. Let me introduce a simple (yet profound) method for applying the principles of information ethics to the moral dilemmas you will no doubt encounter in your lives. There are four steps to the method, shown in Table 1.2.

The *first step* is to get the facts straight. This is obvious but crucial. We cannot make good judgments without adequate information. The *second step* is to identify the moral

---

Table 1.2

The Four-Step Method of Principled Ethics

1. Get the facts straight.
2. Identify the moral dilemma (inspect the facts in light of your moral feelings).
3. Evaluate the moral dilemma using the principles of information ethics to decide which side has the most ethical support.
4. Test your solution: will it stand up to public scrutiny?

---

dilemma by reviewing the facts in light of your own conscience and gut feelings. The concept of a dilemma is important here. Dilemmas are good–good conflicts, which means that you are faced with a choice between two equally acceptable (or good) courses of action. Most of our everyday moral choices involve conflicts between bad and good options (either steal the CD or don't steal it, for example), which are relatively easy to resolve. It is much more difficult to resolve a true dilemma that requires us to turn away from one moral position for the sake of another one. Tough moral dilemmas are becoming more frequent due to the complexities of new information technologies. That is why we need ethics—to help us resolve these more complex problems. The *third step,* then, is to evaluate the moral dilemma in light of the four principles of information ethics. It is helpful to keep a tally sheet and assign each principle to one side or the other in the good–good conflict. Which side has the moral edge? You can make that judgment by determining which side has the most principles supporting it. It would be an ideal world if we could always uphold every principle that we have an obligation to uphold. Unfortunately, in the real world where we live, it is sometimes necessary to choose between our principles. Principled ethics helps us make that kind of choice less painful by promoting the practice of never overriding one principle unless other principles support such an action. Finally, the *fourth step* is to test your solution by asking this question: Would I still be satisfied if my decision (or behavior) were reported for all to see in the *New York Times*? I can illustrate how this method works by discussing the real-life case of Lotus Marketplace: Households.

On April 10, 1990, Lotus Development Corporation and Equifax announced their intention to sell a CD-ROM product that they were developing.[11] Lotus is a software company best known for its Lotus 1-2-3 spreadsheet; Equifax is one of the three major credit bureaus (TRW and Trans Union are the other two). The product they were developing was called Lotus Marketplace: Households. It was going to be marketed to small businesses that wanted the opportunity to expand their customer base through direct-mail advertising. The CD-ROM product would consist of a software program and a list of five thousand potential new customers. The projected cost was $695, with the option of purchasing additional lots of five thousand names for $400. The lists would be generated from Equifax's Consumer Marketing Database, which maintains profiles on approximately 120 million individuals and 80 million households. Included in a Marketplace: Households profile would be a person's name, address, gender, age, marital status, shopping habits, and income level. Also included would be categories for lifestyle information, such as "inner-city singles."

Suppose you owned a small luxury-car dealership in Portland, Oregon. For $695, you could purchase the Marketplace: Households CD-ROM, then use the list of five thousand names to mount a direct-marketing campaign. Your list of names would match the profile you specified. For example, you might have specified an age limit of older than 40; a minimum income of $60,000; an address in Washington, Clackamas, or Multnomah counties of Oregon; and a propensity for buying luxury items.

On January 23, 1991, Lotus and Equifax withdrew their product before it had ever reached the market. They canceled Marketplace: Households because of the controversial response it elicited. Thousands of people wrote angry letters and E-mail messages to Lotus's corporate headquarters in Cambridge, Massachusetts. They felt that the product would transgress their personal privacy. The companies had hired a privacy consultant in an earlier stage of development and had built privacy safeguards into Households. For example, they did not provide telephone numbers with their customer profiles to ensure that people on the list would only be contacted by mail, which is less intrusive than a telephone call. In addition, the product was going to be sold only to legitimate businesses and would include a carefully worded contract prohibiting the resale of any names. Consumers would also be given the opportunity to have their names excluded from the lists.

Critics were not satisfied with these safeguards, however. How could Lotus guarantee that the information wouldn't be resold? Purchasers of Marketplace: Households would be permanent owners of the lists. Would the information be accurate a year later? Was it accurate in the first place? How could consumers withdraw their names from lists already sold? These concerns (and others) fueled the fire until the companies canceled the product. Was cancellation the best moral course of action? That is the question we want to answer in this illustration of the four-step method of principled ethics.

The first step is to get the facts straight. It helps if you ask yourself this question: Who are the parties with something at stake here? The stakeholders are (1) the companies that are trying to create and sell the Households product, (2) the smaller companies that will benefit from inexpensive access to a list of potential customers, and (3) the consumers about whom private and even very personal information is being sold.

The second step is to identify the moral dilemma by inspecting your own moral feelings. It seems to me that most Americans don't have a problem when credit bureaus like Equifax collect private information, then sell it to banks and other creditors that use it to gauge their risk before lending financial assistance. Businesses have a legitimate need to protect themselves. But should this private information, which is legitimately used to aid potentially risky decision making, also be available for marketing purposes? It is one thing to review a credit report in order to determine someone's ability to pay back a debt. It's something quite different to review a credit report in order to determine someone's predisposition to buy your product. In

21

the first instance, the customer initiates the transaction and gives at least tacit permission to have his or her credit investigated. In the second instance, the customer does not play an active role and is subject to perhaps unwanted solicitation. Here is the moral problem according to my gut reaction: Is it legitimate for Lotus and Equifax to sell essentially private credit reports for advertising purposes? The good–good conflict pits legitimate business practice (credit reporting and advertising) against the right to privacy. Ideally, we would want to uphold both sides, but in this case, that didn't happen.

The third step is to evaluate the moral dilemma with the four principles of information ethics, then make an informed decision about which side has the moral edge. (This will make more sense after you read the chapters on each principle; I'm only illustrating how the method works at this point.) The first principle is respect for intellectual property, which reminds us that, in our society, we honor the practice of making a profit from ideas and invention. Clearly, this principle will support the entrepreneurial efforts of Lotus and Equifax. The second principle is respect for privacy, which reminds us that, in our society, we also honor a personal need for autonomy that would not be possible without some control over what others know about us. This principle supports the customers in the Marketplace: Households case just as clearly as respect for intellectual property supports the companies. So far, we have been able to restate the moral dilemma as a case of respect for intellectual property versus respect for privacy. Just doing that much isn't enough, however. There are two more principles to evaluate. If we can determine that one side of this case has the support of additional principles, then we will be able to assess the moral worth of the decision to cancel Marketplace: Households.

The third principle is fair representation, which reminds us that we do not tolerate deceptive business practices in this society. This principle does not seem especially relevant to the case because Lotus and Equifax are not trying to deceive anybody about what their product can and can't do. There is probably weak support for the customer side of the dilemma since some of the claims about Marketplace: Households might not be feasible even with the best intentions. For instance, it is hard to imagine how the companies could guarantee all customers an option to remove their names from the database. What if you were out of town when they tried to contact you? Finally, the fourth principle is nonmaleficence, which reminds us that we also don't tolerate harmful business practices in this society. I believe this fourth principle supports the privacy claims of the consumers in the Households case. The customers were particularly offended by the fact that the lists would be the permanent property of anybody who purchased the product. Not only was this an abridgment of their privacy, it seemed to be a harmful invasion of privacy. So the two principles working together—respect for privacy and nonmaleficence—are necessary in order to capture the full force of the moral feelings being expressed.

Tally the results and you see that at least two principles support the consumer side of the dilemma and only one principle supports the company side. Based on that evidence, it is reasonable to say that Lotus and Equifax did the right thing by withdrawing their product from the market.

That does not mean a similar product, with different privacy safeguards, won't eventually become morally acceptable to the American public. Direct-mail advertising is widely practiced, and certainly the larger companies already purchase credit-report information for their advertising campaigns. But Americans have every right to expect that private information about them will be handled in a careful, moral fashion. As we shall see in chapter 3, private information is an extension of our own personhood and should be treated as such by companies wanting to sell private information.

The last step in the method of principled ethics is to test your decision by imagining that it will be reported in the *New York Times* for all the world to see. Does that possibility change your thinking in any way? Publication is a way of universalizing your decision, which often brings perspective and a little more objectivity. In this case, I don't think more perspective would change matters. In real-life situations of moral crisis, however, you will need an opportunity to step back and let your feelings subside. That is the purpose of this last step.[12]

The method of principled ethics that I've just illustrated hinges on the ability to interpret moral apprehension (my "gut feeling" or squeamishness tells me something is wrong here) as a red flag marking an unresolved conflict. You need to practice identifying such conflicts and determining whether they are true moral dilemmas (conflicts involving good versus good options rather than the more familiar good versus bad options). Normally, only the good–good conflicts are complex enough to require ethical evaluation. As a homework assignment, you might try to find one example of each type of moral conflict (good–bad and good–good) in the newspaper.

Finally, I want to reiterate the simplicity of principled ethics. The four-step method is simple enough to incorporate into everyday life. Ethics is often presented as an overly complex discipline, which defeats its purpose. The purpose of ethics is to serve our morality. It helps us become better moral agents because it enables us to resolve difficult problems that tend to overload and then stifle our morality. Like Forrest Gump, we want to be profoundly simple in our response to the complexities of the information age. But we don't want to be simplistic, settling for rigid, morally exclusive answers. Ethics is a persuasive, reasonable discipline that encourages us to be flexible and open to new options. It requires that we give consideration to all of our allegiances, not just one (or even two). The only rule in ethics is that you can't disregard an important principle unless more principles of equal importance will support such a position.

When you have finished reading the chapters that follow about each of the four principles, be sure to investigate the case studies presented in the appendix. It will be your opportunity to practice using the method of principled ethics outlined above.

Summary

We live in a world that is permanently more complex because of our increased technology dependence. Information technologies in particular—telephones, television, CD players, computers, the Internet—have increased the likelihood that our wakeful time will be filled with externally stimulated activities. As a result, internally stimulated activities such as moral reflection are likely to suffer from neglect unless a conscious effort is made to practice them.

Unfortunately, the kinds of moral problems we face in the information age are becoming more complicated at the same time that we are becoming more externally preoccupied. One way to stimulate or boost our moral capabilities is to turn to ethics. Morality pertains to the personal sense of right and wrong that we derive from our upbringing; ethics, on the other hand, pertains to the principles that stand behind our morality and make it effective. Bringing ethical reflection to bear on our moral problems makes them less difficult to resolve.

One of the most effective ethical applications is the method of principled ethics. By keeping in mind the four essential principles of information ethics (respect for intellectual property, respect for privacy, fair representation, nonmaleficence), we are better able to resolve the good–good moral conflicts that we face with more frequency. The four principles also remind us that we have multiple allegiances that are not easily dismissed. Moral exclusiveness—settling for the simplistic answer—is not an option with this method. Simplicity is important because principled ethics is meant to be incorporated into our everyday morality. The method has four steps: get the facts straight; inspect your moral feelings and identify the dilemma; evaluate the dilemma with the principles of information ethics and come to a moral conclusion; test your judgment against public opinion.

For Further Thought

In 1842, Russian author Nikolai Gogol published the novel *Dead Souls*.[13] It is the story of Pavel Chichikov, a minor government clerk who discovered a foolproof way to get rich quick. Chichikov quit his job, bought himself a fine carriage, and began traveling to the rural regions of Russia to put his plan into effect. He would arrive in a new village, tell people he was a vacationing landowner, then wait for the inevitable invitation to dine with the local nobility. Chichikov was pleasant and entertaining; wealthy people liked him and invited him to stay at their homes. Finally, Chichikov would act on his scheme by asking his new friends whether any of their serfs or farmhands were recently deceased. Of course, every large estate would have at least a few such "dead souls." Chichikov offered to buy them, explaining that it would be a last opportunity to earn at least a few pennies back from their loss. The landowners thought it was a peculiar request but usually complied in order to please Chichikov, who seemed so eager to have them. That is how Chichikov became the owner of an estate with fifty thousand souls. He knew from his previous work that it takes at least a year for the names of the dead to be removed from government records. So Chichikov acquired a bogus estate of the newly deceased, then applied to the government for a mortgage using the dead serfs as collateral. His get-rich-quick scheme worked.

Chichikov's scheme hinges on the value of information. He was able to make a fortune because he knew how to "market" his insider's knowledge of the government. Try to think of some similar immoral tales that captured the news headlines recently. In the nineteenth century, Gogol's story was sensational; today, it is rather common. Is there a difference between stealing a chicken, for example, and stealing a sentence or some other unit of information? What, if anything, makes the information age unique and different? Please pause and think about these moral questions.

Notes

1. Darwin, *Voyage of the Beagle,* 217.
2. Kohák, *Embers and Stars,* 1–26. Kohák reflects on the consequences of life in a world dominated by electronic technologies. He claims that electric lights have banished the night sky from our life experience, which, surprisingly, weakens our moral capabilities. I mention this book because it seems that we haven't really thought about how technologies that are invented to help us can also change us in profound ways. See Edward Tenner's *Why Things Bite Back* for a more recent discussion of the often harmful consequences of technological innovation.
3. Howard, *Death of Common Sense,* 1–53.
4. Morrow, "Yin and Yang, Sleaze and Moralizing," 158.
5. Beauchamp and Childress, *Principles of Biomedical Ethics,* 3–24. Beauchamp and Childress discuss the four basic principles of biomedical ethics: respect for autonomy, nonmaleficence, beneficence, and justice.
6. Kidder, "Tough Choices," 30.
7. Edney, "Lament for a Shipmate," A19.
8. See the bibliography at the end of this book if you want to study

ethics in more theoretical detail; the entries for Aristotle, Jonas, Kant, Kohák, Mill, Nussbaum, and Rawls are particularly noteworthy.

9. Howard's complaint in *Common Sense* is that laws are like rules but should be based on principles. He argues that common sense is a form of principled judgment that is dying because we've cluttered our lives with too many rulelike laws that preclude the possibility of exercising judgment.

10. *Forrest Gump,* directed by Robert Zemeckis (Paramount Pictures, 1994).

11. Spinello, *Ethical Aspects of Information Technology,* 136–40; Mason, Mason, and Culnan, *Ethics of Information Management,* 9–11. The Marketplace: Households case has been widely discussed in recent information ethics literature; the two sources listed here are especially helpful. Daniel Seligman's article "The Devil in Direct Marketing" provided a good discussion of the case in the national press.

12. Immanuel Kant (1724–1804) is the philosopher who made the argument that we should test our morals against universal opinion. He said that we know we've behaved morally only when our actions would be acceptable for everyone. In *Ethical Decision Making and Information Technology,* Ernest Kallman and John Grillo discuss five different versions of this kind of universal moral test. My *New York Times* test is similar to what they call "the TV test."

13. Gogol, *Dead Souls,* 29–48.

Chapter 2

Respect for Intellectual Property

To own a home—furnished according to one's individual tastes—is part of our cultural heritage. We believe that our chances for happiness in life are greatly enhanced by such ownership. We also believe that ownership is linked to our labors (or the labors of our forebears); the harder we work, the more money we earn, the more able and deserving we are of property. Our moral sense of fairness would be disturbed if the link between effort and ownership were overturned. We think of property ownership as a natural right fully protected by both moral conscience and the laws of the land.

Not all property is as physically tangible as homes, cars, and dishes. Intellectual property refers to intangible things

31

such as poems, chemical formulas, and mechanical designs that can be "owned" as well. The concept of intellectual property is especially dependent on the cultural conviction that creative labor merits compensation. It is the creative effort of invention that confers the right of ownership for intellectual property. The poet owns the poem because he or she labored to write something original.

Since the Middle Ages, Western societies have attempted to protect intellectual property rights through legal means. The primary mechanisms for such protection are trade secrecy, copyright, and patent laws. The legal protection of intellectual property has always been commercially motivated. Individuals willing to invent new ways of doing things, or new expressions of thought and human feeling, were protected from competitors who might try to imitate them. But legal protection is not meant to be permanent. Patent protection only lasts for seventeen years in America, whereas copyright protection lasts for the lifetime of an author plus fifty years. Inventors, authors, and publishers are given a temporary monopoly—a head start on their competition—which potentially rewards them for their originality and risks.

The information age has put enormous stress on the legal mechanisms for protecting intellectual property. The biggest problem so far has been how to deal with computer software. Computers themselves are not difficult to protect since they are clearly machines, which fall under the domain of patent law. But what is software? Is source code (the software program as written in BASIC or some other programming language) a literary work, like a poem, and therefore deserving of copyright protection? Or is it like a trade secret—an electronic version of Colonel Sanders's secret recipe for tasty fried chicken? Is object code (the machine-readable version of the source code) merely an integral part of the computer that deserves patent protection like the computer itself? Or finally, is the algorithm (the flowchart that depicts the logical steps for accomplishing a task that is the basis for the source code) like a mathematical proof, which is unprotectable by law because everyone has a right to use reason and clear thinking?

Software does not fit into the categories of prior intellectual property law. It is something new and different. One legal scholar described software as "a machine whose medium of construction happens to be a text."[1] This confusion about software—is it a patentable machine, or is it a copyrightable text?—has led some lawyers to suggest that it would be best to start over from scratch and invent a new legal category for information age products. Such a dramatic change is very unlikely, however.

Trade secrecy, copyright, and patent laws are slowly being upgraded to fit our more complex, high-tech times as judges make case-by-case decisions. One of several such cases that we shall investigate later in this chapter is *Apple* v. *Microsoft*. Until a clear consensus emerges from the litigation process, there will be considerable ambiguity about what is and is not protectable intellectual property. This is where ethics can help.

In the past, our moral sense of fair play was largely in tune with intellectual property laws. For instance, it made good sense that an author who signed a contract with a publisher wouldn't go out shopping for a second or third publisher for the same book. We didn't (and still don't) need to consult a copyright lawyer in order to appreciate that the first publisher has the right to make a profit from the risk it takes for publishing the work. But now there is a growing gap between the law—which is itself in a confused state about some aspects of the information age such as software—and our moral instincts. Why is it that so many people feel no moral restraint about copying proprietary software, music CDs, and the like? It is as if the law had lost touch with ordinary life, which makes the law easier to disregard. I believe this gap between our moral instincts and the law is an unfortunate cost we pay for living in a complex technological society. My contention in this chapter is that ethics can help us to bridge the gap between our moral instincts and the still-emerging intellectual property laws by reminding us of our obligation to respect intellectual property.

Morality, Ethics, and the Law

I believe there has been a temporary reversal in the order of our inner compulsions to do the right thing. If I don't steal a music CD when the opportunity arises because my conscience tells me it would be wrong, that is a *moral* compulsion. On the other hand, if I don't steal the CD because I fear being caught and punished, that is a *legal* compulsion. The ideal society is one in which citizens refrain from murder and theft because such acts are immoral, not because they are illegal. If our only restraint were legal compulsion, then life would become nightmarish as lawmakers and lawyers frantically tried to plug up every conceivable avenue to crime. In normal circumstances, the law works best in response to morality, building on the prescriptive moral framework that provides a strong sense of right and wrong. Instead of law following the lead of our morality regarding intellectual property rights, however, we have the reverse situation.

Unfortunately, evidence suggests that our morality is not responding effectively to the prescriptive and often confusing legal restraints concerning intellectual property. According to the Business Software Alliance (BSA), the software industry—which accounted for $36.7 billion of the U.S. economy in 1995—is losing approximately $15 billion per year to software piracy. The BSA also estimates that one out of every three software programs currently in use was pirated. More than any other group, computer professionals should appreciate the high costs of software development and the harm piracy does to a company that has invested millions of dollars in research and development. Yet half of the information systems professionals who participated in a *Computerworld* ethics survey said they make illegal copies of commercial software. Software piracy has become the equivalent of jaywalking, according to one writer.[2]

Jaywalking is a good analogy because it illustrates the gap that can grow between the law and personal morality. Many communities have outlawed jaywalking and determined what kind of fines offenders should pay. But it is a law that is rarely enforced. People don't feel criminal when they cross the street in a nonauthorized fashion; it's not the kind of behavior that stirs up deep moral guilt. Without moral cooperation and assent, laws tend to be ignored. It does not matter whether the law in question is trivial (such as jaywalking) or important (such as copyright infringement). If the law does not have the support of personal morality, it will not be effective. This is a lesson the information age needs to learn.

The solution to so-called victimless crimes of the information age—software piracy, unauthorized access to databases, electronic theft—is not more laws or higher fines. Instead, it would be better to close the gap between what the law requires and what our moral instincts say. We have a moral crisis here, not a legal one. Many Americans have determined that because high-profile companies such as Microsoft are owned and managed by billionaires, it is not truly harmful to make illegal copies of their expensive software products. We might think of this kind of deliberate indifference to the law as a Robin Hood effect. Some Americans have also determined that it is never wrong to lend personal property to a friend, even if it is a software disk that is not supposed to be lent. When we buy something, we have a right to dispose of it as we wish. This is a deeply held conviction in our society, and the peculiar restrictions of information age licensing agreements seem to be fighting an uphill battle against that common moral background. It is also true that people sometimes break the law simply out of ignorance. Understandably, we are not always sure what constitutes legal use of information and software. In the end, law—like ethics—must follow morality or it is beside the point. There is no other way to police the human heart than by moral persuasion.

In order to narrow the gap between morality and the law, we must turn to ethics, which has an edifying function. The

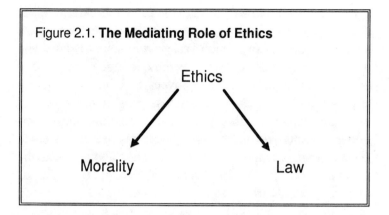

Figure 2.1. **The Mediating Role of Ethics**

purpose of ethics, recall, is to make our morality more effective. Respect for intellectual property is an ethical principle that can enhance the common goals of intellectual property law and our moral instincts. It is similar enough to the law to be able to remind us of it, and it is similar enough to our morality to be able to boost it into action. Principled ethics, in this instance, must stand halfway between the law and morality. Let us very briefly review the rudiments of the law regarding intellectual property—trade secrets, copyrights, and patents—so that an understanding of the law can be incorporated into this important ethical principle.

Trade Secrets

A trade secret is confidential information such as a recipe, algorithm, or manufacturing process that enables a company to maintain its competitive edge. Remember the dinosaur embryos that were stolen by the computer nerd in

Jurassic Park?[3] How to coax extinct DNA back into life is (or would be) a huge trade secret! Trade secrets are protectable by contract law, which varies from state to state. The two most common forms of secrecy contracts are nondisclosure agreements with employees and licensing agreements with customers. Nondisclosure agreements restrict what an employee can say about the company during employment and even after employment has been terminated. The contract usually specifies the topics about which the company expects the employee to be quiet. Breaches of the agreement are prosecutable as felonies. Licensing agreements or leases allow customers to use a company's product under special conditions that protect its secrets. The licensing contract might specify that no reverse-engineering efforts can be made in order to discover how a product works or what its programming entails. As with nondisclosure agreements, breaches are prosecutable as felonies.

Trade secrecy was the earliest form of legal protection in the computer and software industries.[4] It seems to work fairly well in the development stages of a product. It is more difficult to protect secrets once a product is put on the market. Mass-market products such as software programs are especially difficult to protect through licensing. It is also rather difficult to prosecute and win trade secrecy cases of either type (involving employees or customers). Incontrovertible evidence of wrongdoing is hard to collect, yet it seems to be a requirement in order to get a conviction in this arena. Once a secret has been revealed, by illicit means or not, it is part of the public domain and can no longer be protected.

Copyrights

A copyright protects the unique expression of ideas found in an author's creative work. The distinction between an idea and its expression is critical yet sometimes ambiguous. If I write a poem about the blueness of the sky, copyright does not allow me and me alone to speak about the color of the sky. That the sky is blue is the idea about which I have written a poem; everybody else is still free to speak of and write about that idea as well. What copyright protects is the specific words that I use, such as this line: "The blue sky is a disarming tickle to my sober mood." If somebody else writes a poem and copies that expression exactly, or nearly so, then I could sue for copyright infringement. In order to win the case, I would have to prove that the other poet had access to my poem and deliberately copied it. Copyright does not protect my work against someone's independent creation of similar or identical expressions. Copyright protection of literary works such as novels, plays, poems, and software code lasts for the lifetime of the author plus fifty years.

Copyright is the most pervasive form of legal protection in information age industries such as the software industry. The relevant federal laws are the Copyright Revision Act of 1976 and the Software Copyright Act of 1980. As we shall see in the next section of this chapter, there is considerable ambiguity concerning copyright protection of software. Unfortunately, the distinction between an idea and its expression does not always make sense with regard to software programs. The law is slowly evolving and adapting to that fact on a case-by-case basis.

Another ambiguity with respect to software copyright has to do with the tacit analogy many people make to the bookselling business. Prepackaged software is sold in retail outlets such as Egghead Software or Comp USA that are modeled after bookstores. You go into the store, browse the shelves, then pay for what you pick out. Yet the purchase of a software program is not the same as the purchase of a paperback. When I buy a paperback, I am free to lend it to a friend after I finish reading it; when I "buy" a software program, I really only license it for my particular use. Lending it to a friend is forbidden. So there is a subtle confusion that works against our appreciating the differences between a high-tech licensing agreement and an ordinary book purchase.

Not everything with regard to software copyright should be ambiguous, however. It is not proper to lend copyrighted software disks to a friend so that he or she can make a "free" copy. There is no doubt that that sort of behavior is illegal. It is also immoral because we have an obligation to respect laws that reflect our cultural heritage of property ownership. For centuries, rights of ownership have been extended to include the creative expression of new ideas. A rule of thumb to keep in mind with the principle of respect for intellectual property is, simply, "one program per machine." In other words, think twice before you copy any software program on more than one computer; unless you have a multiple-site license agreement, odds are good that it will be illegal and immoral to do so. It is also clearly illegal and immoral to copy the source or object code of a copyrighted program without permission.

Patents

A patent provides the inventor of a new process, machine, or compound with a legitimate monopoly on the use of the invention. Patents last for seventeen years and provide the strongest legal protection for intellectual property. Competitors are forbidden from using, making, or selling the invention for the period of patent protection. The application process for a patent is rigorous; the invention must pass difficult originality tests and fall within strict subject-matter guidelines. There is considerable debate about the value of granting patents to software and other information age products.[5] The debate revolves around the intended purpose of patents.

Since their initial use in medieval Italy, the purpose of patents has been to enhance society by promoting the advancement of technology and science.[6] Patents give inventors an incentive to share their ideas and inventions by offering patent holders a limited monopoly. That enables others to look at the invention and make improvements after the period of protection expires. The more people attempting to improve on the technology and science of a society, the more likely it will flourish; that is the idea behind patent law. With regard to software and similar information technologies, the worry is that, if too many patents are granted, the creative and competitive process of advancement will be stifled. Individual companies holding patent monopolies would get rich, but society as a whole would lose its competitive edge. Because software originates as an algorithm designed to carry out some specific task, it is closely associated with mathematical proofs and mental processes that are not patentable. Ideas, including mathematical proofs and algorithms, are essential building blocks of technology and science that must be freely shared by all for the common good.

The Look-and-Feel Cases

In March 1988, Apple Computer filed suit against Microsoft Corporation, claiming that Windows version 2.03 (and subsequently version 3.0) infringed Apple's copyrights regarding the Macintosh's user interface. *Apple* v. *Microsoft* is the highest-profile case in a series of cases that have contested the extent to which copyright law protects the intellectual property of software developers. They have come to be known as the "look-and-feel" cases. "Look and feel" refers to the nonliteral (or noncode) aspects of a program such as how it looks on the screen and how it feels to navigate with keystrokes and mouse. In order to respect intellectual property at the moral level, we must be able to appreciate the dynamic, uncertain, and evolving status of American law. The law is not simply the handmaid of billionaires and corporations. Judges are attempting to find the razor's edge that will balance the often competing needs and concerns of individuals, companies, entire industries, and society as a whole. Their work is morally praiseworthy. By staying open-minded and supportive of the judges, we can raise our own moral consciousness regarding intellectual property.

Apple v. *Microsoft* is an epic tale because these two companies personify the computer revolution and its stepchild, the information age. Steven Jobs and Stephen

Wozniak, both college dropouts, founded Apple in 1976. They built their first computer in Jobs's garage in California's Santa Clara Valley. By 1980, when Apple went public, it was generating more than $100 million in annual revenues. William Gates and Paul Allen started Microsoft in 1975 after Gates dropped out of Harvard. They moved to Albuquerque and wrote a programming language for the first commercially available microcomputer. In 1980, IBM hired Microsoft—now based in Seattle—to write the operating system software for its new PC. Short on time, Microsoft bought QDOS (Quick and Dirty Operating System) from a Seattle engineer for $50,000 and renamed it MS-DOS (Microsoft Disk Operating System). When Microsoft went public in 1986, Gates became the PC industry's first billionaire. Jobs and Gates in particular defined the new genre of computer nerd turned tenacious, inspired, even ruthless entrepreneur.

Without question, copyright protects the source and object code of a software program. The legal problem has been to determine what additional, "nonliteral" aspects of the program can be protected as well. The door was opened wide for controversy when in 1986 the Third Circuit Court of Appeals affirmed the *Whelan* v. *Jaslow* trial court decision.[7] Jaslow Dental Laboratory, a Pennsylvania denture and prosthetics company, hired Elaine Whelan to design a computer program for its business operations. Using EDL language, Whelan developed a program called Dentalab, which she and Jaslow marketed to other dental laboratories. Later, Jaslow developed a similar program called Dentcom that was written in BASIC language rather than EDL. Jaslow switched to BASIC because EDL code was not accessible to the personal computers used in small dental laboratories. Whelan sued Jaslow for copyright infringement, claiming that Dentcom functioned similarly to Dentalab and used some of the same data and file structures. Jaslow did not deny studying Dentalab but insisted there was no copyright infringement because the literal code had not been copied. In deciding for Whelan, the court stated that copyright protection was available for the structure, sequence, and organization of a program and not just its literal code. The court compared the nonliteral structure of a computer program to the detailed plot of a novel, which is protectable by copyright.

Inspired by the *Whelan* case's expansion of copyright protection for software, Apple sued Microsoft in 1988. But five years passed before the judge could finish his preliminary evaluation of all the complicated issues and set a trial date. In the meantime, the *Whelan* opening for look-and-feel protection had been effectively limited by other cases. *Brown Bag* v. *Symantec* was especially significant in closing the door on *Whelan*. Brown Bag Software bought an outlining program from John Friend, an independent programmer, in 1987. As part of the purchase deal, Brown Bag granted Friend a license to use 129 pages of source code that generated user interface displays. Coincidentally, Friend also developed and sold a different outlining program to Symantec Corporation. In 1988, Brown Bag sued Symantec for copyright infringement, submitting a list of seventeen different features that were allegedly similar. The district court ruled in favor of Symantec in each of the seventeen instances. In its appeal, Brown Bag claimed that the court had focused exclusively on analytic dissection of the user interface, neglecting to evaluate the overall look and feel of the two programs for substantial similarity. The Ninth Circuit Court of Appeals upheld the district court's ruling against Brown Bag.

The *Whelan* case opened the door for broad protection of the nonliteral aspects of software by advocating a gestalt or holistic test for determining similarities between programs. The *Brown Bag* case at least partially closed the door for broad look-and-feel protection by advocating a feature-by-feature dissection test for determining similarities. The dissection test has become more important for at least two reasons. First, it more accurately reflects the complexities of software programs. They are not reducible to only one functional idea, as the judge in the *Whelan* case assumed. Software programs entail expressions of many ideas and must be evaluated accordingly. Second, it is more faithful to copyright tradition, which requires originality in order for protection to be granted. Just doing the work of writing a new program is not enough; the work must also be clearly original. The feature-by-feature dissection approach makes originality harder to demonstrate because so much of programming is functionally limited. How many ways are there to represent a table of graphical icons, for example? Originality implies that something be nonobviously unique, which is not possible if function and convention preclude all but a few options.

By the time the judge in the *Apple* case had evaluated 189 instances of alleged similarity between the Macintosh and Windows interfaces, *Brown Bag* and other similar cases had already established the importance of the dissection approach. Most of Apple's 189 citations of infringement were dismissed because of a secret 1985 lease agreement between the two companies. Most of the remaining allegations were also dismissed because it was determined that Apple had not been the original inventor. For example, the graphical user interface (GUI) feature of displaying multiple windows in an overlapping fashion was first developed by Xerox Corporation at its Palo Alto Research Center. Apple was not allowed to claim copyright protection for features it clearly did not invent. The *Apple* case was dismissed in June 1993, a victory for Microsoft and limited copyright protection for nonliteral elements of software programs.

Slowly but surely, the law is responding to the sometimes new and confusing problems of the information age. Judges are actually boosting the law, making it more effective and relevant, in the same principled way that ethics boosts our morality and makes it more effective. Committed to respecting intellectual property, we have an ethical obligation to hang in there with our legal system. That does not mean we must become copyright lawyers in order to maintain our moral bliss. But we do need to be tolerant of the temporary ambiguity in the law; we also need to be willing to evolve morally as our culture and its legal systems evolve.

Problems on the Way to Being Digital

As the founder of the innovative media lab at MIT and a columnist for *Wired* magazine, Nicholas Negroponte is a digital celebrity. True to that calling, he celebrates "being digital" as if it were a new life-form or force of nature.

Being digital means that bits—the 0s and 1s of computer language—are replacing atoms as our most significant unit of exchange.[8] Instead of publishing paper books and selling them in retail stores (shuffling "atoms" of paper, ink, money, etc.), the coming digital world will allow us to download an electronic manuscript to every networked computer for a fee that is charged to an on-line bank account (shuffling "bits" of computer talk). Peering ahead, I imagine that convenience marketing will be fiercely contested in digital existence. Who can provide the easiest, least inconvenient means of bit transaction? Newfangled wallet PCs will probably be programmable to do our electronic shopping and other necessary chores while we sleep. The easy life of Riley is just around the corner. Or is it? There will be problems on the way to being digital, if that is our destiny. Some of them are already apparent, such as the difficulty of defining intellectual property rights once digital information becomes a universal commodity.

Information is nothing new—it's as old as the hills. But the value of information has increased because being digital makes it more accessible and powerful. Prior to invention of the printing press in the fifteenth century, written ideas were carefully transcribed by hand and stored as one-of-a-kind manuscripts in vaulted monastic libraries. Only a few privileged monks and courtiers had access to the manuscripts. Most people could not read anyway. The printing press made mass production of books possible. For the first time in human memory, average people could afford to own a book and learn to read it. Access to the printed word made modern Enlightenment dreams of universal education and democratic liberties possible. The fact that most of us can read, write, and determine (to some extent) what we want to do with our lives is a consequence of the printing press. Digital information is being hailed as another leap forward in human potential, the next step beyond the printed word. I believe this potential is very real for two reasons.

First, digital information shares the characteristics of mental phenomena—thoughts, feelings, words—more than any other form of written communication. The computer is analogous to the brain; for example, both rely on electrical exchanges to transmit information. Digital information can actually mimic the mind and therefore interact more directly with it. When we sell or trade digital information, we are selling something akin to our own mental processes. Digital information is a new kind of mental commodity. Selling written ideas in traditional book form provides only indirect access to an author's mental processes. We are separated from the author's mind by the mediating activity of writing down certain thoughts while ignoring others. On the other hand, in its capacity for mental mimicry, the computer makes it possible to overcome the formal distance that the structured discipline of book writing places between an author and his or her readers. Californian Ted Nelson's thirty-year odyssey to build Xanadu—a digital library of hypertextual links that allows the reader to jump from one text to another in imitation of the mind's ability to jump from one thought to another—is an ambitious illustration of the potential convergence between digital information and the human mind.[9] The World Wide Web's HTML programming language is a less spectacular, but workable, example of Nelson's dream.

Second, digital information is becoming almost as fluid and plentiful as the electrons upon which it rides, making it an irresistible force for worldwide change. There is no way for governments to stop the exchange of digital information across their borders when it is transmittable by satellites, CD-ROMs, laptop computers, and a host of other high-tech means. As a result, the world is becoming one market and, to some extent, one culture. The global nature of digital information is a potential force for human rights. Consider the flap over Kathie Lee Gifford's Wal-Mart clothing line in the summer of 1996. Gifford, a television celebrity, was chastised in the media because clothing bearing her name was made by American and Honduran women in horrible sweatshops. Nike and other sporting goods companies have come under similar criticism for allegedly exploiting children in Pakistani factories, where soccer balls are made. We have the potential to know what crimes are being committed at any time in any place; we have the potential to insist that every person on the planet be treated with respect.

The potential for both good and evil in the digital world is awesome. At the very least, we run the risk of making ordinary life more stressful and complicated. Bombarded by digital information from all quarters, how are we supposed to sift through the junk and discern what is good and useful? Information overload is a common and serious problem these days. More to the point in this chapter is how to control the use of all this information so that intellectual property owners will not be shortchanged. The same characteristics that make digital information so novel and revolutionary—fluidity, ubiquity, mind-likeness—also make it easy to steal and copy without detection. If I download a copyrighted graphical image from a World Wide Web site, who would know? Would such an act be harmful to the company that created the image? Is it realistically possible to outlaw something I can do in the privacy of my home?

In September 1995, the Bill Clinton administration issued its white paper outlining policy goals for intellectual property and the national information infrastructure. According to one legal scholar, the white paper's strong advocacy of anticrime measures favors the rights of commercial publishers almost exclusively.[10] The white paper overlooks the traditional dual purpose of intellectual property law, which is to enhance society and the free exchange of ideas while at the same time providing publishers and other creative marketers with limited protection from imitators. How to stop high-tech intellectual property crime might be getting more attention than it deserves. We also need to worry about how the fair-use doctrine of copyright law applies to the information age.

Fair-use doctrine protects the often overlooked societal aspects of copyright law by ensuring the right of researchers, teachers, and ordinary citizens to use copyrighted materials freely for specific purposes. For example, fair use allows a writer to quote up to three hundred words from another author's copyrighted work without first getting permission or paying a permissions fee. It also allows teachers to present and discuss copyrighted materials in the classroom. Photocopying put a temporary strain on fair-use practice, though case law has clarified the situation. Suppose you want to read a magazine article at the public library. You could sit down and read it there, or you could make a photocopy and take it home to read later. Under fair-use guidelines, it is acceptable to photocopy articles—even books—if the photocopy is for temporary personal use. On the other hand, it would not be acceptable to make ten photocopies and distribute them at your PTA meeting.

I believe we must allow for adequate fair-use opportunities and not assume that the law only protects commercial interests. Earlier, I suggested that a rule of thumb to keep in mind with the principle of respect for intellectual property is "one copy per machine." The rule reminds us of the moral obligation to refrain from pirating software, which inhibits small companies in particular from marketing new products because they cannot be assured of a fair return on their investment. Here is a second rule of thumb to keep in mind with respect to digital information: "download for temporary personal use only." Whereas the first rule of thumb highlights the commercial side of intellectual property law, the second rule of thumb highlights the societal or fair-use side. It reminds us that, in most cases, it is morally acceptable to copy material from the Internet or an on-line resource if our intention is to use it privately. This rule only applies under the assumption that initial access to the digital information was itself aboveboard. In other words, it is not morally acceptable to download articles from the *New York Times* for private use if, first, you hacked your way into the *Times* database. Having paid for on-line access, or used a subsidized account such as a library might provide for free, then it is proper to download for later personal use.

Downloading for temporary personal use, like photocopying, is often morally acceptable because it does not interfere with a company's ability to publish and disseminate an information product as it sees fit. If you infringe on the distribution prerogatives of a digital publisher, on the other hand, you will probably be on shaky moral and legal ground. Creating hot links on the World Wide Web, which direct users to other Web sites, is an example of a potentially illegal practice. Hot links are a problem because they can determine how people perceive a digital resource and how they gain access to it, which interferes with the publisher's right to determine such matters for itself. If I publish a book that republishes material from other books, then I need to get permission to reuse the other material. Publishing a Web page that consists of hot links to other digital resources is a form of republication that probably ought to require permission as well.

Rather than fret about copyright infringement, some companies are changing how they do business in order to take advantage of the downloading capabilities of potential customers. Consider the story of Netscape Communications Corporation, which gives away its best product for free. Netscape was founded in 1994 by Silicon Valley legend James Clark, who formerly had founded Silicon Graphics.[11] The company created an Internet software program—Netscape Navigator—which allows users to browse the World Wide Web. The browser is available for free on the Internet. Netscape went public just seventeen months after its inception, and its stock has risen through the roof. With 85 percent of the browser market, Netscape has become an industry standard. Now the company is selling its line of server products to corporate clients, which will allow them to communicate and conduct business on the Internet. Netscape is a multibillion-dollar company that got started by encouraging Internet users to download its product and give it a try.

Summary

Intangible things such as poems can be "owned" in much the same way that houses, cars, and other tangible things are owned. Trade secrecy, copyright, and patent law traditions evolved as mechanisms for protecting the rights of intellectual property owners. These traditions are being stretched to the limit in the information age due to the increased importance of intellectual property. Software in particular seems to eclipse the categories of prior intellectual property law. In these confusing times, ethics can play a mediating role between morality and the law. Respect for intellectual property is an ethical principle that captures the gist of the law while at the same time reminding us of our moral obligations.

Apple v. *Microsoft* is a high-profile look-and-feel case that illustrates the effort to make copyright law more relevant to the computer age. Apple claimed that Microsoft's Windows operating system infringed its copyrights for the Macintosh desktop. The *Whelan* v. *Jaslow* trial had opened the door for broad, nonliteral copyright protection of software, but *Brown Bag* v. *Symantec* helped close the door. Apple lost its suit because the judge used *Brown Bag*'s dissection test for determining similarities between the software programs. The dissection test exposed the nonoriginal and functional nature of key aspects of the Macintosh GUI that were not covered by a prior secret lease between the companies.

Our lives are becoming more digital, which means that the transfer of computer bits is replacing the transfer of atoms as our most important transaction. Digital information is more valuable and powerful than previous forms of information because it is more mindlike, plentiful, and unstoppable. One key problem with digital existence is how to protect intellectual property when it is so easy to download and copy computer files. President Clinton's recent white paper on intellectual property seems preoccupied with stopping criminals and ignores the fair-use doctrine that promotes the educational, noncommercial values of the law. Two rules of thumb help recall the dual purpose of intellectual property protection. First, "one copy per machine" reminds us of the moral obligation to honor the commercial interests of innovative companies by refraining from software piracy. Second, "download for temporary personal use only" reminds us of the moral right to copy digital information for temporary personal use if it will not interfere with the publisher's right to control distribution.

For Further Thought

1. In 1987, Robert Post, a former automated teller machine (ATM) repairman, was arrested for stealing $86,000 from New York City ATMs.[12] He spied over the shoulder of ATM customers in order to steal their personal identification numbers (PINs), and collected discarded receipts in order to steal their account numbers. Then he made bogus ATM cards at home with a machine that he bought for $1,800. Post was caught

---

after an ATM machine had been programmed to signal guards when a faked card was being used. When questioned about his crime, Post said that he was a "white-collar criminal," not a mugger and thief. He was surprised that the bank wanted to prosecute him instead of hiring him as a consultant to prevent further ATM theft.

Post seemed to think that white-collar crimes are not harmful in the same way that crimes against real people are. Does his distinction have any moral merit, or was it just self-serving? Post's surprise at not being offered a job suggests that he had little or no remorse over what he did. Why do you suppose he lacked moral compulsion?

2. When IBM managers hired Microsoft to create an operating system for its new PC in 1980, they had no inkling that software would eventually become more lucrative and powerful than the computer itself. Otherwise, IBM would have developed its own software, and there never would have been a Microsoft Corporation. But software represents a new kind of product, and it took us a while to realize that.

Software is unique because it can transform the functionality of a computer. What a computer can do—hence, what it is—is determined by the software that tells it how to operate its electrical switches. If hardware is comparable to the human body, then software is the mind. Both are necessary, but the mind is the control center. By controlling the control center, software companies have stolen the limelight away from the traditional manufacturing giants. Prior to the computer age, products comparable to the human mind were simply not possible.

Mindlike products have increased the value and importance of intellectual property and digital existence; they have challenged the relevancy of copyright law in particular. How has our morality been affected by this change?

Notes

1. Randall Davis, as quoted in Samuelson, "Case Study," 306.
2. Blalock, "Don't Copy That Floppy," 46; Greenberg, "Getting Tough on IS Crime," 27; Betts, "Dirty Rotten Scoundrels?," 101.
3. *Jurassic Park,* directed by Steven Spielberg (Universal Pictures and Amblin Entertainment, 1994).
4. Samuelson, "Case Study," 284.
5. Ibid., 301–4.
6. David, "Intellectual Property Institutions and the Panda's Thumb," 44.
7. Samuelson, "Case Study," 296–99.
8. Negroponte, *Being Digital,* 11–20.
9. Wolf, "Curse of Xanadu," 138.
10. Samuelson, "Intellectual Property Rights and the Global Information Economy," 23–29.
11. Bottoms, "Jim Clark," 12.
12. Forester and Morrison, *Computer Ethics,* 15.

Chapter 3

Respect for Privacy

In 1987, President Ronald Reagan unsuccessfully nominated Robert Bork to the Supreme Court. The televised confirmation hearings were heavily contested by Democrats, who questioned Judge Bork's weak stance on personal privacy, among other topics. Ironically, an overzealous reporter managed to acquire a list of videos that Bork had rented, which his employer then published. This invasion of personal privacy—nobody needs to know what kind of videos a judge or any other citizen watches—was widely condemned. Within a year of the Bork hearings, a law prohibiting disclosure of video rental information was signed by the president.

In 1996, computer consultant Aaron Nabil-Eastlund created a Web page that publishes the Oregon Department of Motor Vehicle's database matching license plate numbers to names and addresses of car owners.[1] Nabil-Eastlund felt that Oregonians would drive more responsibly if they knew that other drivers could find out who they are on the Internet. Too much anonymity, he thought, leads to irresponsible behavior on the roads. If other drivers know who you are and where you live, you'll think twice about being discourteous. Within a week of publication, this cybervigilante's Web site had attracted thousands of visitors. The governor called and helped convince him to shut it down at least temporarily. Many people don't want their names and addresses available to the public; occasionally (in stalking cases, for example), people's lives may depend on their anonymity.

Unfortunately, stories about how information age databases endanger personal privacy are becoming commonplace. It is likely that we all know someone whose credit has been compromised by misinformation or tampering. Our medical records are shared by insurance companies. It is getting to the point where we can't buy anything or go anywhere without being tracked and categorized by sophisticated marketers; we leave junk mail trails that prove it. At work, our phone conversations or E-mail messages (if we use E-mail) have perhaps been monitored by somebody. More than one hundred different federal agencies gather information about us and store it in their separate computers. Heaven help us if and when they put aside interagency competition and collate all their files. Would any of us be able to recognize the detailed data portraits of ourselves and neighbors that the government owns?

One-third of Americans reported being concerned about

invasion of privacy in 1970, at the dawn of the information age. Half of us had become concerned about privacy by 1977, and four out of five of us by 1990.[2] This trend is understandable when you consider that personal information about each one of us is transferred from computer to computer an average of five times a day.[3]

Computer databases have almost infinite storage space, making it convenient to keep permanent records of everything, including the videos we rent. Databases are also easy to search, which enhances their ability to display complete records within seconds. Database records are especially easy to change and copy; so far, hackers have had little problem gaining unauthorized access to the proliferating mountains of sensitive computer data. Technology enthusiasts believe that encryption will solve the invasion of privacy problems that our increased reliance on computers has temporarily caused. Encryption is a mathematical encoding system that makes data unreadable without a secret key.

Certainly, we need encryption and other technology enhancements to ensure that sensitive information remains secure. But privacy issues in today's complex world go much deeper than that. Privacy enables us to develop as individuals with unique histories and stories. What happens when too many other people take control over my story? This is a key personal identity problem we face in the information age. In this chapter, I demonstrate how important it is to think about what privacy means to us. The ethical principle of respect for privacy should remind us to be moral advocates for privacy safeguards in the marketplace, work setting, and government agencies.

Morality, Ethics, and the Law

In the last chapter, we saw how the principle of respect for intellectual property mediated between morality and the law. Mediation was necessary because of the growing gap between complex intellectual property law and common-sense morality. With privacy, we have a different set of circumstances, requiring a different conception of how ethics, morality, and the law are related. There is no strong legal tradition extending back to the Middle Ages in the privacy arena as was the case with intellectual property.

The Fair Credit Reporting Act of 1970 is illustrative of the piecemeal approach to the legal protection of privacy in America. Among other things, this law requires credit agencies to make their records available to the people about whom they issue reports, and it stipulates procedures for correcting false information. It is a good law as far as it goes, but it is limited to just one industry—the credit-reporting industry. By necessity, there are more than two dozen other federal privacy laws that regulate different sectors of American society, such as electronic funds transfer, debt collection, and cable communications. The closest thing we have to a comprehensive law is the Privacy Act of 1974, yet it only stipulates what federal government agencies must do to protect individual privacy. This piecemeal approach has created a confusing, complicated system with many holes and oversights. This is a different kind of problem than what we saw with regard to intellectual property law.

The difficulty with intellectual property law has been how to make trade secrecy, copyright, and patent traditions fit into the new and complex world wrought by computer technology. The traditions are slowly being updated as judges make decisions in cases such as *Apple* v. *Microsoft.* On the other hand, the difficulty with privacy law has been how to establish a common standard for the protection of privacy in all sectors of society. This is slowly happening as more and more piecemeal laws are passed to cover specific issues such as video rental records. The need for privacy protection has grown considerably in the information age, just as the need for more technical intellectual property protection has grown. Yet these similar needs are being met differently because of their different legal prospects.

As we also saw in the last chapter, morality is playing catch-up in the intellectual property arena, where the law seems to have left many of us behind. The ethical principle of respect for intellectual property is supposed to help us care more about companies that sell software and other high-tech products that are easily pirated. Morality has a different role to play in the privacy arena, on the other hand. We must take more of the initiative for change upon ourselves in order to achieve comprehensive privacy protection in American society. Remember what happened in the Bork case. First, Bork's privacy was invaded by the reporter who obtained the list of his rented videos; next, there was a moral outcry against such behavior; finally, Congress quickly passed legislation that ensures the privacy of video rental records. The ethical principle of respect for privacy should encourage us to insist on adequate privacy safeguards. If we express moral concern—even outrage— as many did in the Bork case, eventually we will have comprehensive privacy protection.

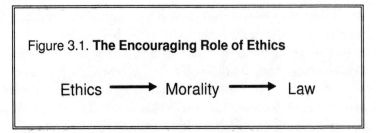

Figure 3.1. **The Encouraging Role of Ethics**

Ethics ⟶ Morality ⟶ Law

As Figure 3.1 suggests, the principle of respect for privacy must boost our morality so that we will become more informed and proactive about privacy matters. It is *our* privacy that is at stake, and it is up to us to make our concerns known. Lawmakers should follow our moral lead in these matters and not the other way around.

AT&T is a large corporation that has taken the moral initiative in setting its own high standards for privacy protection. Every employee is required to take personal responsibility for the privacy and security of phone conversations (and other transmissions) that the company brokers for its clients. Here are some of the guidelines to which employees must adhere:

- Don't tamper with or intrude upon any transmission.
- Don't listen to or repeat conversations, and don't permit them to be monitored.
- Don't use information from or about any communication for personal gain.
- Don't disclose information about consumer billing arrangements or the location of equipment to unauthorized people.[4]

Other companies and professions have been equally innovative and morally responsible about privacy concerns. Equifax, the credit-reporting company that codeveloped the Marketplace: Households product discussed in chapter 1, began conducting an annual survey on privacy in 1990. By responding to consumer concerns expressed in the survey, the company is building credibility and earning consumer trust. Equifax also established a twenty-four-hour, toll-free access line for obtaining a personal credit report and discontinued the practice of selling lists derived from its database to direct-marketing companies.

The library profession has a long history of protecting the borrowing records of its patrons. In fact, once a book is returned, all traces of who checked it out previously are deleted. In most library automation systems, it would not be possible to generate an electronic list of the books that Judge Bork or some other citizen borrowed; such lists don't exist so that the privacy of library users can be honored and protected. These are just a few examples of how ethics and morals, rather than the law, can motivate us to do what is necessary to protect the privacy of our clients and neighbors. It makes good business sense to treat people respectfully and to assume that personal privacy is a matter of importance to them.

Finally, I want to mention the five goals for privacy protection that were outlined in a 1973 government report called the "Code of Fair Information Practices." It has served as a model for subsequent privacy legislation and should continue to do so. It can also serve as a primer for the ethical principle of respect for privacy. Let these five goals be concrete reminders of what privacy protection must entail in a high-tech information society:

1. No secret data record-keeping systems should exist.
2. People must be given the opportunity to find out what information is recorded about them and how it is used.
3. People must be given the opportunity to prevent personal information from being used for purposes other than what it was originally collected for.
4. People must be given the opportunity to correct records containing information about them.
5. Organizations that create and use personal records must assure the reliability of the data and take precautions to prevent its misuse.[5]

Stories R Us

Bill Gates is building a house in Seattle that will keep track of guests who wear a personal identity pin.[6] The pin will transmit each guest's whereabouts to a computer database with records about the personal tastes of Gates's friends and other potential guests. When a pinned guest enters a room, the lighting, climate control, music, and other house systems will make subtle adjustments to please and satisfy the guest's known tastes. Electronic panels built into the walls will even display digital art that suits each individual.

I suspect that most of us would enjoy being guests at the Gates house just because it would be a unique, interesting experience—like a world's fair exhibit or a carnival fun house. If such tracking devices as the "personal pin" were the norm in our society rather than a curious exception, it would probably not be a fun experience, however. The Gates house would then be more reminiscent of George Orwell's 1949 novel *Nineteen Eighty-Four*.

Winston Smith is the unfortunate hero of Orwell's satire

about totalitarianism in technological society.[7] Smith worked for the Ministry of Truth as a correctional writer; he rewrote the government's (Big Brother's) three-year progress plans so that their predictions always came true. His life was monitored by Big Brother's two-way telescreens, which were everywhere. Smith started to keep a secret journal when, by chance, he found that he could be alone and unobserved if he skipped lunch. He wrote hateful things about Big Brother in his journal, which surprised him and made him feel afraid. Then he met Julia, another disgruntled citizen of Oceania, and became her lover. They were caught reading subversive materials by the Thought Police and tortured. The book ends when the brainwashed Smith finally understands how much he "loves" Big Brother.

It is instructive that Smith's initial rejection of Big Brother happened only after he was able to enjoy a few private moments alone. Like Smith, we would be mere pawns in the hands of others if we could not set aside time for daydreaming and making plans. Privacy, or personal freedom, is the basis for self-determination, which is the basis for self-identity as we understand it in American society. Too much monitoring by Big Brother—or the boss or the marketers who say they mean well or the government— compromises our ability to have identities that are self-determined.

"Who are you?" If someone asked me that startling question, I would probably tell a short or long version of my personal story. If the questioner were someone I had never met before, my response would be brief: I was born and raised in South Dakota, I graduated from the University of

65

Iowa, I work at Marylhurst College in a suburb of Portland, Oregon. These are some of the bare facts of my personal story. If the person asking me who I am were already known to me, a more detailed version of my story would be told. The point is that self-understanding is always conceived as a narrative. We are the stories that we tell about ourselves; we cannot make sense of our lives without saying something about our beginnings, struggles, triumphs, and pending demise, as the world's great literature attests.

Personal data collectors—marketers, government agencies, employers, creditors, insurance companies, health organizations, and the like—are building extensive digital profiles about each one of us. As more details get added, these profiles become powerful unauthorized "biographies" that can compete with our own abilities to tell the story of who we are. That is what happened to a Houston schoolteacher when someone stole her good credit history and ran up so many bills that she was denied a home mortgage.[8] It happened to a Los Angeles resident who couldn't find an apartment to rent because she had mistakenly been labeled a troublemaker by a company that sold information about renters to landlords.[9] I believe we must have some degree of freedom from the scripts of others in order to be self-determining. That is certainly one of the moral lessons of *Nineteen Eighty-Four:* when Big Brother has more say about who I am than I do, then the very notion of individual self-identity is lost.

The principle of respect for privacy can sensitize us to this peculiar self-identity issue in the information age. More specifically, respect for privacy demands that two safeguards, at minimum, be established to protect the self-

authoring prerogatives of each of us. First, it is imperative
that database owners get permission before using private
information for secondary purposes. In Oregon and many
other states, for example, the Department of Motor Vehicles sells information about its citizens to marketing firms.
The DMV doesn't ask for permission to reuse personal information given in good faith for a specific purpose—to
register vehicles and pass a driver's test, as the law requires. Instead, the DMV assumes that it "owns" the information and can therefore sell it as a product. I believe that
is an immoral assumption because it unnecessarily in-
fringes upon the ability of citizens to be the masters of their
own destinies. In some instances, such as wartime, we must
give up our personal freedom for the greater good of de-
fending our country. It is doubtful that the resale of private
information for marketing purposes constitutes such a com-
pelling greater good for the DMV, however.

Second, it is imperative that database owners provide
people with convenient, free opportunities to correct inaccuracies in their personal profiles. It is unfortunate when
someone's life is interrupted by a false credit report or
some other electronic mistake. Errors are inevitable, though
we must do all that we can to minimize their consequences.
Ideally, database managers should query each person about
whom they have records at least once per year. Send a free
copy of their profile and invite them to make changes if
they find inaccuracies. Inform them about what uses are
being made of their records and ask for their consent. The
right to self-determination in a free society demands that
much.

We must learn to think of personal data as an extension

of the self and treat it with the same respect we would a living individual. To do otherwise runs the risk of undermining the privacy that makes self-determination possible. Remember that when we gather private information about people, we are constructing rudimentary stories. Out of moral respect, we must defer to the self-authoring prerogatives of free citizens. We must also learn to think of personal data as never more than "co-owned" by database owners, thereby ensuring that individuals will always have an important voice in what gets said and sold about them.

Make It a Policy

In 1989, Nissan Motor Corporation hired Bonita Bourke and Rhonda Hall to run an E-mail network for its Infiniti operation in Carson, California.[10] Their job was to train dealers to use E-mail as an alternative to the U.S. mail, telephone, and fax. Management heard that the women were exchanging love letters on the company's E-mail system and began to monitor them. The women were admonished about such behavior and warned that they could be fired, which is what happened after Bourke and Hall filed a grievance for invasion of privacy.

The issue of E-mail privacy has been one of the most visible and controversial workplace problems of the information age. Many employers think of E-mail systems as a business tool owned by the company and made available for employees to use for work purposes only; they often assume that E-mail messages, like receipts and correspondence kept in filing cabinets, are the sole property of the company. Employees, on the other hand, typically think of the E-mail system as a communication device similar to the telephone; they often assume that it is available for both work and personal use and that their messages are private property. These differences in perception between some employers and most employees have led to problems and lawsuits. In order to correct any false assumptions on the part of employees, and avoid misunderstanding about their privacy rights, employers ought to publish an E-mail policy.

An E-mail policy should be brief, clearly written in plain English, and widely disseminated so that everyone is aware of it. It should address the following issues at least, using examples whenever possible to dispel ambiguities:

- What the purposes of the E-mail system are and how it should be used.
- Under what conditions, if any, employee E-mail is available for personal use.
- Under what conditions, if any, employee E-mail will be monitored, and by whom.
- Whether employee E-mail will be archived or copied for permanent storage.
- What the consequences are for misuse of the E-mail system.
- What recourse employees have for complaints about E-mail monitoring or privacy concerns.

If you need guidance in drafting a policy or wish to study several different sample policies, you may want to contact the Electronic Mail Association.[11]

Some companies—such as General Motors, McDonnell Douglas, Warner Brothers, and Citibank—have made E-mail completely private. They have policies of never monitoring employee E-mail under any circumstances. Other companies—such as Epson, Eastman Kodak, Du Pont, UPS, and Pacific Bell—have reserved the right to examine employee E-mail.[12] If you are not sure what the policy is at your workplace, be on guard. It is safest to assume that your E-mail is not private and secure. Avoid using anger, humor, irony, or all capital letters in E-mail messages because they can be easily misinterpreted.

Contrast what happened to the women who worked for Nissan with the happy ending Bill Gates describes concerning his E-mail–enhanced romance at Microsoft. Nissan fired Bourke and Hall for allegedly writing love letters; Gates has said that many romances at Microsoft—including the courtship of his own wife, Melinda—were helped by the company's E-mail system.[13] Which company atmosphere would you prefer? This is a moral issue, and I believe the principle of respect for privacy tips the scales in favor of Microsoft's atmosphere for two reasons. First, it is more consistent with the privacy expectations that most Americans have regarding their phone conversations, U.S. mail, and other similar forms of communication, including E-mail. Why contradict that expectation? The advent of computer-based telecommunications has made life in the information age complicated enough without making further distinctions that are counterintuitive.

Second, it seems like a good opportunity to demonstrate trust in employees by respecting their judgment not to let personal E-mail use interfere with work. It is unrealistic to assume that people can suspend all references to their personal life while at work or vice versa. My guess is that some of the best insights good employees have about their work first occur to them at home. An employer that wants loyal, hardworking employees should think twice before establishing policies that might seem harsh or rigid.

The Electronic Communications Privacy Act of 1986, while outlawing third-party interception of E-mail, unfortunately does not provide clear protection against employers that monitor the E-mail of their employees. Short of pressing for societal unanimity on this issue through the law, we must minimally require clearly defined company policies. We can also put moral pressure on employers to be mindful about how important privacy is to a healthy sense of self-identity.

E-mail privacy is just one example of the broader problem of workplace privacy. Advanced technologies have made it easier to monitor employee performance. For instance, there are software programs that enable supervisors to count the number of keystrokes that employees make on their computers. Many data-entry workers must average so many keystrokes per minute in order to keep their jobs. There are also software programs that allow supervisors to observe what an employee has on his or her computer screen.

How much of this digital supervision (or "dataveillance") is appropriate? When does it become overly intrusive and disrespectful to the employee? How realistic is it to evaluate performance based on simplistic quantitative data? These are moral questions that we will be debating

71

for some time to come. In the meantime, it is imperative that employers be honest with employees. If performance is being monitored electronically, then say so in a written policy that is clearly worded and widely disseminated. Policies are critically important because the automated workplace is a relatively new experience for most of us. Our expectations are not yet settled, and they often vary according to how well we understand computers. Employers must take steps to ensure that everybody understands what they are expected to accomplish and how they will be evaluated.

I believe the high-tech workplace is becoming more and more comparable to the research setting in hospitals and universities. Every research institution that receives federal grant money must have a policy handbook that outlines the procedures for protecting the privacy and dignity of people who voluntarily become the subjects of scientific research. The safeguards are painstakingly administered in order to ensure that subjects understand the risks they are undertaking and the potential benefits. Deceptive or distressing experimental designs—for example, having someone administer an electrical shock to animals in order to test the human capacity for sadism—are rejected as immoral. Employers could learn a great deal about how to treat their employees from the ethical handbooks of the research community. Their basic premise is that, in order to be happy, people require autonomy (or self-determination) as well as the private space to exercise it. How much autonomy and privacy are required to ensure employees a reasonable chance for happiness in their work? More than some employers seem to think, I wager.

Summary

Our personal privacy is under siege in the information age because computers make it easy to store and retrieve data about practically everything. Marketers, creditors, insurance carriers, employers, and government agencies have amassed extensive records about each of us. One problem is how to keep all these personal data profiles out of the wrong hands. Encryption is being heralded as a high-tech solution to this security issue. On a deeper moral level, the erosion of privacy threatens our sense of personal identity.

American law has taken a piecemeal approach to privacy protection, making it difficult to afford consistent and comprehensive attention to this issue. Ethics can help make up for the lack of comprehensive legal protection by encouraging us to be strong moral advocates for personal privacy. Companies such as AT&T and Equifax can serve as examples of moral advocacy for privacy rights. They earn the trust of their customers by taking measures to ensure their privacy, which probably enhances their business prospects as well. The principle of respect for privacy can remind us of the five goals for privacy protection outlined in the "Code of Fair Information Practices": don't keep secret records about people; allow them to know what records are being kept and how they are used; allow them to decline the use of personal information for secondary purposes; allow them to correct mistakes; and don't allow personal records to be misused.

If "Big Brother" denied us all personal privacy, our self-identities would be destroyed just as Winston Smith's was in Orwell's *Nineteen Eighty-Four*. Privacy is one of the necessary ingredients of self-identity. We are the stories that we live and tell about ourselves. The profiles about us that data collectors "own" are rudimentary stories that compete with our own abilities to say who we are. It is imperative that we understand how the erosion of privacy threatens our self-identities; that is where the principle of respect for privacy can be of the most benefit. In order to protect the self-authoring prerogatives of each one of us, respect for privacy demands at least two safeguards on the part of database owners: (1) that they get permission before using private information for secondary purposes; and (2) that they provide people with free opportunities to correct inaccuracies in their records.

E-mail privacy is a controversial workplace issue. Some companies have determined that E-mail should be used for work purposes only, and they are willing to monitor employee E-mail to ensure that the system is being properly used. Other companies, on the other hand, have allowed employees to use E-mail for personal as well as work purposes, and they usually guarantee that the E-mail system will not be monitored. Given this divergence in E-mail system management, it is imperative for employers to publish E-mail policies that inform employees about their privacy rights. Most employees have an expectation that E-mail is a private form of communication, like telephone calls, which adds to the moral importance of a policy that states to what extent E-mail is in fact private. Published policies are a good idea for other matters of privacy in the automated workplace as well. If you monitor employees' work output on a computer, then tell them up front that you are doing so. The ethical considerations shown for the privacy and dignity of research subjects can serve as a model for the digital work environment.

For Further Thought

1. In 1989, Epson America hired Alana Shoars to administer the E-mail system at its Torrance, California, facility.[14] Her job was to increase E-mail use so that the company could save money on its long-distance communication costs. It is much cheaper to send an E-mail message across the country than it is to send a fax or telex. When Shoars took the job, 48 percent of the Epson employees were using E-mail; after nine months, she had raised the number of users to 98 percent. In part, Shoars encouraged more employees to use the E-mail system by convincing them that their messages would be as confidential as traditional U.S. mail. She told them that nobody at the company had access to their secret passwords, which ensured the privacy of their E-mail accounts. Shockingly, Shoars discovered that her supervisor was intercepting the company's E-mail as it passed through an electronic gateway from Epson to MCI. He had stacks of copied E-mail messages on his desk. Shoars confronted him about this breach of privacy, which contradicted her assurances in the E-mail training sessions. She was told to mind her own business. Instead, she took her complaint to the CEO. A short time later, Shoars was fired. Two lawsuits against Epson by Shoars were unsuccessful.

Consider your own expectations about E-mail.

Should a company be allowed to do as it pleases with employee E-mail, as the Electronic and Communications Privacy Act seems to allow? It seems that Shoars's supervisor was dishonest for allowing her to tell employees that their E-mail was confidential when it wasn't. What can be done about such apparent dishonesty? Should there be legal consequences for immoral behavior?

2. Suppose you work in the marketing department of a company that has just adopted a stringent privacy policy. Included in the new policy is a promise to customers that efforts will be made to get their permission whenever personal information about them (such as income level) is used for advertising. Your boss is understandably worried. She asks you to design a mass-mailing strategy that would advertise a product, advise customers about their choice to participate in the ad campaign, and control costs. After some preliminary work, you decide that the most direct and thorough strategy would be to send potential ad campaign participants a stamped, returnable postcard with a check-off box if they want to opt out. This would also be the most expensive and time-consuming option, however. An alternative strategy that you consider is to include a statement at the bottom of a mail advertisement that informs customers of their right to be withdrawn from the campaign if they so desire. But in this case, it is up to the customer to take the initiative and incur the expense to write a letter if he or she wants out.

This strategy doesn't add to the expense of the campaign. But is it enough to satisfy the moral intentions of the new policy? Is a "passive" opportunity for privacy protection—leaving it up to the customer to take action—as good as an "active" opportunity whereby the company takes all the initiative? Take a moment to think about this issue.

Notes

1. Oliver, "Oregon Vehicle Owners Pop Up on Internet," A1.
2. Eder, "Privacy on Parade," 39.
3. Ibid., 38.
4. Ibid., 40.
5. Johnson, *Computer Ethics,* 96.
6. Gates, *Road Ahead,* 214–26.
7. Orwell, *Nineteen Eighty-Four,* 3–48.
8. Forester and Morrison, *Computer Ethics,* 89.
9. Ibid., 91.
10. Wiegner, "Trouble with E-mail," 46.
11. In 1991, the Electronic Mail Association published a report that analyzes the advantages and disadvantages of four different policies. The report can be purchased by sending $45 to the Electronic Mail Association, 1555 Wilson Blvd., Arlington, VA 22209.
12. Casarez, "Electronic Mail and Employee Relations," 39.
13. Gates, *Road Ahead,* 143.
14. Alderman and Kennedy, *Right to Privacy,* 310; Bjerlkie, "E-mail," 14–15.

Chapter 4

Fair Representation

Several of Jane Austen's novels have been made into successful films recently. Austen's stories are about nineteenth-century English manners. In *Pride and Prejudice,* for example, she examines the ignoble motives that often lurk behind gossipy judgments of a person's character.[1] As Elizabeth Bennett discovers, much to her own chagrin, Mr. Darcy's reputation for snobbishness is undeserved. Instead, he is a man of too few words and too little spontaneity, perhaps, which are faults of a sort, but not anything so seriously wanting in a good man's character as the vice of pride. In fact, it is Miss Bennett's prejudice—her willingness to believe what others tell her about Mr. Darcy without adequately testing their judgments first—that becomes the moral object lesson of the story.

I believe that Austen's novels are especially appealing at this time because many of us have a sense that good manners are no longer taught and affirmed. Unfortunately, life seems less civilized now—less well mannered. One obvious indication of our lack of civility is the increased incidence of lawsuits. We sue one another over practically everything, whereas in Austen's stories, disputes are resolved in a social context that supports personal honor above all else.

It may seem a bit surprising, but the same moral framework of honesty and honor that undergirds Austen's nineteenth-century agrarian society also undergirds our own world of high-tech commerce. Vendor–client commercial exchanges are based on trust and promise keeping. When we buy a product—a software program, let's say—we are trusting the company that made the software program. Specifically, we trust that the company is selling us something that will work as advertised or promised in its promotions and warranties. If the program has too many bugs, we expect the manufacturer to do something about it. Without this pregiven commitment to honesty and service, business practice as we know it would not be possible.

As life has gotten more complex in the twentieth century, more and more laws have been passed to buttress the basic moral framework of business practice. Liability law in its various categories now stipulates degrees of responsibility for manufacturers and service vendors. Ironically, liability law itself has become so complex and all-encompassing that its original purpose—to help ensure that honesty and moral integrity will be honored in the complex business world—has been swallowed up and forgotten. In big business, especially, it seems that people are more concerned about what the law requires than about what conscience requires.

When the law becomes more important than morality, that is a sure sign of trouble. Conscience is a much better motivator than threats of legal judgment; apparently, the law doesn't inspire honesty (as conscience does) so much as it inspires a desire to use the law for one's own gains. I believe that we have created a legalistic society in America that is less moral than it ought to be because the law has unwittingly gone into competition with morality and made it expendable. As a result, we rely too often on lawyers to resolve all our problems. Nowhere is this more obvious than in business.

The ethical principle of fair representation can help swing the pendulum back toward morality slightly, so that the law isn't overburdened with trying to police every conceivable situation in which dishonesty might occur. "Fair representation" refers primarily to the manner in which vendors make their products and services known to clients. In the fiercely competitive culture of high-tech business, there is often an unbearable temptation to deceive clients about what a product can do ("tell 'em what they want to hear") or what its limitations are. Often, the pressures to make a sale (and in doing so, keep one's job) eclipse the propensity to be honest that one derives from a good upbringing.

There is no better portrayal of the grim realities inherent to a life in business than Arthur Miller's *Death of a Salesman*. Miller's play tells the sad tale of Willy Loman, an old, deluded, discarded salesman who determines that the only dignified way left for him to help his family is to kill himself for the insurance money. When the stakes are so high, morality is sometimes viewed as a luxury that is beside the point. Perhaps it is this sense of the futility of morality in the face of life's hardships that has led to an over-reliance on the rule of law. When competition gets so fierce that honesty seems superfluous, then laws limiting how far one might rise or fall seem particularly warranted. Accountability is one of the limitations of morality in comparison to the law: there is no way to guarantee the moral honesty or goodness of others except through persuasion. We need both kinds of compulsion—inner and outer, moral and legal—in a complex society such as ours, but the pendulum seems to have swung too far toward the legalistic side.

Despite its limitations, morality plays a vital, necessary role in business and should never be overlooked or displaced. Quite simply, companies that are committed to honesty, noncoercive sales practices, and good service do better in the long run than companies that follow the path of minimal compliance with the law. Honesty is a moral precept, not a legal one. If you have designed a software program to help raise sheep, don't sell it to the gullible rancher who wants to use it to raise horses. Fair representation reminds us to be moral advocates on behalf of our customers when they are naive. If you want to avoid lawsuits and keep your customers happy, treat them with moral fairness.

According to one astonishing survey, 75 percent of all software that is in development never makes it to the marketplace.[2] That means information age companies must be very careful about when they begin promoting new products. There are many famous instances of "vaporware"— that is, computer products that are announced too soon and sometimes never make it to market. Ted Nelson's *Xanadu* is the granddaddy of them all, introduced in the 1960s and still (apparently) forthcoming. Less vaporous, though perhaps not much less significant morally, were the two- and three-year delivery delays for Microsoft's Windows 1.0 and Lotus's graphical version of its 1-2-3 spreadsheet. Fair representation is an ethical reminder that we must beware of unique high-tech moral issues such as vaporware. It should also remind us of the special duties that information technology manufacturers and vendors have toward their customers. When customers invest in expensive computer systems, they are simultaneously investing in the company's future ability to service their systems and keep them updated. As we shall see in this chapter, customers of high-tech products are especially vulnerable and subject to the moral scruples of their vendors.

Morality, Ethics, and the Law

In chapter 2 we discussed the problem of applying intellectual property law to new information age technologies—particularly software—that do not fit into previous categories. Is software a machine, and therefore subject to patent law, or is it a written text, and therefore subject to copyright law? Actually, software is a unique hybrid of both types of prior intellectual property. In response to the complexities of information age products, intellectual property law has itself become exceedingly complex. One consequence of this increased complexity is a growing gap between what our moral instincts tell us about good behavior and what the law requires. It was suggested earlier that ethics can mediate the gap between morality and intellectual property law.

The same kind of twofold problem can be seen in the case of liability law, which establishes the legal responsibilities that sellers must meet on behalf of buyers. First, there is some confusion about how to interpret software (once again), the never-before-seen entity that is the backbone of the information age. Is it a product, or is it a service? There are two different legal traditions that cover the liability concerns for these different categories of vendor (manufacturers and service providers). As in the machine versus text controversy, software seems to defy prior legal categories. Generally speaking, canned software that you buy off the shelf is treated as a product in liability law, whereas customized software that is designed for one client only is treated as a service. Mixed types of software (partially canned, partially customized) are treated in a mixed fashion legally: if the problem area pertains to the canned part, then product liability will be operative, and so forth.

Second, an unfortunate gap has also grown between what our moral instincts tell us about vendor–client relations and what the law requires. The law has become so all-encompassing that it seems fair to say that morality is sometimes seen as irrelevant. The irony is that the law's purpose is simply to ensure that moral trust and promise keeping will be honored. So we need to do something about this gap, just as we did with the gap between morality and intellectual property law; ethics can help us to mediate the problem just as it did before. But in this case, the principle of fair representation must play a *recovering* role rather than a strictly mediating one as with the principle of respect

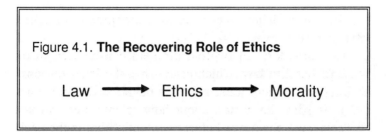

Figure 4.1. **The Recovering Role of Ethics**

Law ⟶ Ethics ⟶ Morality

for intellectual property. We need to recover the moral import of liability law in order to relieve the unrealistic pressures that are put on the legal system. The law can't monitor the human heart; only moral conscience can. Yet we seem to expect the law to anticipate every opportunity for dishonesty in business. That is unrealistic, and it only leads to the nightmarish situation of being overwhelmed by too many laws with too much fine print.

As Figure 4.1 indicates, ethics mediates between morality and the law by playing a recovering role. Specifically, what needs to be recovered is the sense of personal responsibility that undergirds every kind of social intercourse, including client–vendor transactions. In a large, complex society, it is easy to forget that how we treat one another really matters. We cannot rely exclusively on the law to ensure mutually acceptable moral behavior; we need ethics to exhort us as well.

In its recovering role, ethics can educate us about the moral basis for liability law, which should then empower us to treat our customers and business partners with moral respect. When you treat people well, they tend to reciprocate; taking legal action against you would be the last thing on their minds. It is a strategy that works, as Kingston Technology Corporation has demonstrated. Founded in

1987 by John Tu and David Sun, California emigrants from Shanghai and Taiwan, respectively, Kingston Technology is the world's second largest maker of add-on memory modules for personal computers. Tu and Sun treat their employees, suppliers, and customers like family, and it has been the basis for their success. They pay wages that are well above the industry average, and each employee has been promised at least one year's salary should the firm fail. As a result, they have a sales-per-employee average of $2.7 million, which exceeds most of the best-run companies. Kingston Technology never pressures its suppliers about price or cancels orders, and pays its bills ahead of schedule. Because of this civility, and because of the size of its orders, it always gets the best prices and prompt deliveries from hard-nosed suppliers such as Samsung, Hitachi, and Motorola.[3]

Incredibly, Tu and Sun do most of their multimillion-dollar deals on the basis of a handshake. That might be going too far for most of us. What I am suggesting is that a commitment to treat people with moral decency—even kindness—when coupled with contracts and other legal tools, can help restore the trust and commitment to service that are the basis for successful business practice. Restore that moral culture and the frequency of legal actions should recede to a more acceptable level. People respond to kindness and moral consideration. Let me conclude this discussion of morality, ethics, and the law by reviewing briefly the categories of liability that the law stipulates for the sale of products, including computers and canned software. It can help us to appreciate how the law attempts to ensure moral honesty and fairness in the marketplace, and it can serve as a primer for what the principle of fair representation might encourage us to do in order to avoid lawsuits. The categories are strict liability, warranties, and negligence.

Strict Liability

In America, we hold people accountable for the reliability of products they bring to market. Strict liability is the most rigorous form of legal accountability. It provides recourse for people when a product causes harm to them or their property. Strict liability is liability without fault, which means that manufacturers and vendors are held accountable even when the harmful nature of the product could not have been anticipated or prevented. Jim Prince has argued that canned software should be treated in this most rigorous legal fashion because of the positive social effects it promotes. First, strict liability standards encourage software developers to anticipate and control risks in their products, thereby ensuring that great care will be taken before software is introduced to the stream of commerce. Second, strict liability spreads the costs of injury and risk for software products in the most equitable fashion by forcing the developer to include an "insurance" program in the product itself (and its costs). Remember that services cannot be held to strict liability standards. In the case of software, that means that producers of customized products are not strictly liable because such products tend to be thought of as services. Only things that are placed fully into the stream of commerce, such as a Lotus 1-2-3 spreadsheet program that you buy off the shelf, can be considered under strict liability product guidelines.[4] There is no moral way to avoid lawsuits pertaining to strict liability because there is no way to anticipate unintended harms that a product might cause. Strict liability extends well beyond the bounds of moral fairness, but for reasons (mentioned above) that are morally praiseworthy.

Warranties and Disclaimers

There are two kinds of warranties that pertain to the legal protection of customers, implied warranties and express warranties. Implied warranties provide a minimum level of legal protection for every transaction or contractual relationship between a customer and a seller. Specifically, implied warranties guarantee legal protection regarding a product's fitness for its intended purpose and its merchantability. When the vendor knows what the intended purpose of the customer is, the vendor has some obligation to meet that purpose with an appropriate product or system. Merchantability, on the other hand, refers to a product's durability: it must be capable of performing at an acceptable level for products of its kind under ordinary conditions. If a computer system repeatedly fails for no apparent reason, it could be judged not merchantable under implied warranty law. Implied warranties offer some guarantee that vendors will be honest about what they sell us; as such, they offer the clearest example of the law's trying to ensure a moral standard in the business world. How can you avoid suits based on charges pertaining to implied warranty? Be moral, or scrupulously honest with your customers.

Express warranties pertain to issues of product quality

and are part of a written agreement. They usually make promises or guarantees about a product and specify what the manufacturer will do, if anything, when something goes wrong. Increasingly, manufacturers are writing disclaimer statements that are a kind of negative express warranty. Disclaimer statements tell the customer what the limits of the manufacturer's liability are, such as "Microsoft disclaims all other warranties, either express or implied, including but not limited to implied warranties of merchantability and fitness for a particular purpose, with respect to the SOFTWARE, the accompanying written materials, and any accompanying hardware."[5] Disclaimers are somewhat controversial and hold up in court only when they do not exceed what would be considered reasonable. Again, I believe that a strong commitment to treat customers with moral respect and foresight would help to reduce the number of conflicts pertaining to warranties, express or otherwise, that end up in litigation proceedings.

Negligence

Negligence is a failure to exercise due care in something, such as providing a professional service or designing a product. (Whereas strict liability and warranties pertain to product liability but not service liability, negligence pertains to both.) Someone who sues for negligence must prove that the typical standards for doing something—developing a software program, let's say—were not followed. Such carelessness is negligent because a reasonable person buying good software would expect that it was properly designed and tested first. One difficulty with negligence suits regarding information technologies is the relative newness of the industries and therefore the potential lack of adequate standards for testing and development. Without adequate standards, negligence is hard to demonstrate. A moral commitment to do everything one can to make quality products would certainly help in this area. The information technology field is so unpredictable—who knows when the next generation of processors or Internet-accessing tools will spring up and render everything previously available obsolete?—that it becomes imperative to speed up the process of conceiving, designing, testing, and marketing new products. Netscape, for example, was offering its first Web browser for beta testing just a few months after its incorporation. Change of a revolutionary order is happening with such regularity that it's hard to exercise caution or patience (moral virtues of long standing) and still survive. The speed of our times is a big challenge to traditional morality, which evolved in much slower times. Be aware of this challenge and find acceptable ways to be quick, when necessary, *and* moral.

Here a Bug, There a Bug

In the summer of 1994, executives at Intel Corporation were informed that their new Pentium microprocessor had a slight flaw. The Pentium chip, which contains more than 3 million transistor circuits, apparently was missing a few crucial circuits that would allow it to access a lookup table for certain types of mathematical software. One highly publicized consequence of the flaw was that when you divided one large number by another one, the answer was sometimes wrong. In one case, the number 4,195,835 was divided by 3,145,727, then multiplied by 3,145,727. Instead of getting the original number back for an answer, as one would expect, the Pentium chip gave an answer of 4,195,579, which is off by 256. Intel executives decided to fix the flaw on all new chips but to ignore it for those chips already manufactured and sold or ready to ship to customers. They believed that the flaw was so slight that most users would never encounter a problem anyway. Then, in October, a mathematics professor from Virginia published a note about the Pentium glitch on the Internet, which spread quickly and initiated considerable debate.[6]

Intel did not publicly acknowledge that there was a flaw in its chip until November. At that time, the company offered to replace chips only if customers could demonstrate that they really needed an unflawed chip. Late in November, the national media picked up the story. As a result of the bad press, Intel's stock began to fall. Then, in early December, IBM decided to halt its shipments of computers containing the flawed chip. By then, the minor Pentium problem had become a major disaster.

Finally, on December 20, 1994, Intel executives apologized for the problem and announced that they would recall and replace all flawed chips with no strings attached. The only thing customers had to do was call a toll-free number to make arrangements. This action finally ended the crisis that had been building.[7]

Some of the "hysteria" concerning the Pentium chip fiasco was exaggerated media intensity of the kind that preceded Admiral Jeremy Boorda's unfortunate death in 1996 (which was discussed in chapter 1). Much of it, however, was honest moral outrage. According to a *PC Magazine* article, Intel let us down in three ways. First, the company did not acknowledge its error as soon as it knew about the problem; second, it shipped flawed chips even after confirming the problem; and third, it did not move fast enough to assure customers that it would fix the problem by replacing the flawed chip. These observations provide an excellent reminder of what the principle of fair representation ought to teach us.[8]

Honesty is the most crucial moral virtue in every commercial exchange, and it is often the most difficult to practice because of the pressures to succeed—even if one has to cheat. We must not overlook the brutal nature of competition—someone loses, someone else wins; someone goes without a paycheck because the sale didn't go through, someone else gets a bonus for closing the deal—which lends a dog-eat-dog survivalist mentality to some (if not all) business settings. I am reminded of *Glengarry Glen Ross,* an insightful film about the pressures of making a sale in order to make ends meet. The two main characters, one played by Jack Lemmon, are business associates and friends to a point. They will do anything to secure hot "leads"—that is, the phone numbers of likely customers whom they can swindle. Friendship, morality, even legality, lose all meaning because of the overriding necessity to make a sale and get a paycheck.[9]

Given this context, which is amoral at best, it is perhaps understandable that Intel executives would overlook the crucial importance of honesty when they did not immediately communicate the Pentium problem to customers. They were probably doing what was best to protect themselves from competitors. But they forgot to focus on the needs of their clients, which are not based on competition. Instead, the client–vendor relationship is based on moral trust. Once you break trust with your clients, once you step onto the slippery slope of dishonesty, things get bad in a hurry. You find yourself, like Intel, in a speeding avalanche of customer anger and mistrust.

An honest confession in the summer of 1994 would have helped Intel immensely. Perhaps its executives didn't apologize for fear of a lawsuit. My guess is that it didn't occur to them because successful business executives tend to operate out of a competition mind-set first and a moral mind-set second. Exposing one's weaknesses in public could lead to strategic advantages for competitors. Doing business successfully is a highly complicated affair, entailing multiple purposes (competition and service, for example) that often conflict with one another. Nevertheless, it is fair to say that the Intel executives dropped the ball in this case because they failed to recognize the *moral* framework (not the *competition* framework) out of which customer complaints concerning their chip were made. In that context, an apology is most appropriate, as is customer forgiveness once amends have been made.

Not only must we practice honesty in order to create a trusting atmosphere for vendor–client transactions to be successful. We must also take moral responsibility for the consequences of our mistakes. A simple confession in the summer of 1994 would not have been enough to rectify all of Intel's problems. We would also expect Intel to stop shipping flawed chips and to replace the flawed chips that had already been sold. Morality is an *activity* born out of reflection; you have to do something in order to fulfill your moral responsibilities and correct your mistakes.

The *PC Magazine* article I mentioned above draws a contrast between Intel's response to the Pentium problem and IBM's recent response to a similar problem. The author gives IBM credit for immediately recalling its OS/2 Warp program so that it could fix a bug in the installation process. Bugs are inevitable in this era when microprocessors have millions of circuits and software programs have thousands of lines of code; it would be impossible to foresee every conceivable interaction glitch as different programs are thrown together with different processors. The important thing is that major companies such as Intel must react swiftly and responsibly when bugs arise, as IBM did. Despite the risks inherent to doing business in a highly competitive marketplace, honesty about bugs is paramount, as is a willingness to take the necessary actions to fix them.[10]

To its credit, early in 1995, Intel decided to change its policy for disclosing flaws in Pentium microprocessors. Now the company promises to disclose flaws as they are discovered. This is a good move that will enhance the moral reputation of Intel despite the 1994 fiasco.[11]

In a nutshell, the ethical principle of fair representation should boost our sense of moral service on behalf of the customer. Service entails a commitment to make the other person happy first; it is the noblest, most altruistic ideal that is inherent to doing business and making a profit. Naturally, we must not overlook the dark side of doing business in a competitive world where mistakes can cost much, including one's livelihood. But hard-nosed realism must never exclude the moral idealism that also has a basis in human experience. Keeping promises, being honest, and safeguarding the trust that is extended from customer to vendor are essential aspects of the moral calling to service.

Finally, the principle of fair representation can encourage companies to adopt a whistle-blowing policy. If employees are expected to tell the truth, and report situations that seem to compromise the company or its customers, then it would help to have specific written guidelines. The policy should make it clear that an employee who reports something is not being a snitch. The object of whistle-blowing is not to dig up gossip about one's colleagues or to get them fired. Instead, it should be a sounding board for the moral concerns that individuals might have about their work. The confidentiality of such discussions should be guaranteed up front in the policy. It would help if one person was the designated mentor or counselor for such discussions. Think of the tragic explosion of the space shuttle *Challenger,* which might have been prevented had one of the design engineers been able to report his or her concerns about the faulty seals in the fuel tank. A whistle-blowing policy might have encouraged such a discussion, which might have led NASA to cancel the launch. Giving employees an opportunity to express their gut moral feelings in a safe and confidential manner could help to establish a good, positive work culture.

Play It Conservative

American Airlines Corporation's automated reservation system, called SABRE, has been in operation since 1976 and is widely considered the best in the industry. In 1986,

AMR (the information systems subsidiary of American Airlines) decided to exploit its success with SABRE by marketing its expertise to other areas of business. The area that quickly caught AMR's eye was the hotel reservation business. It discovered that only 20 percent of hotel reservations were made through a centralized system, compared to 80 percent for airlines. In collaboration with Marriott, Hilton, and Budget Rent-a-Car, AMR decided to build a multi-industry reservation system—called Confirm—that would handle a client's travel, lodging, and car rental needs in one operation.[12]

Even though Marriott, in particular, already had its own efficient hotel reservation system, the potential benefits of this new state-of-the-art system were enticing. Everyone was aware of the strategic advantages that American Airlines enjoyed because of SABRE's success: other airlines were forced to make their reservations through SABRE or APOLLO (the automated reservation system of United Airlines), and pay a royalty to do so, because they had become the industry standards that travel agencies used. So the reputation of AMR, built on the phenomenal success of SABRE, was crucial in getting the other three companies to commit their resources to such a major undertaking.

To develop something as sophisticated as the Confirm system requires lots of money. The initial contract, signed in September 1988, called for the partners to provide AMRIS (the AMR subsidiary that would develop Confirm) with $55.7 million. The contract also specified that the system design phase would take only seven months and the development phase forty-five months, meaning that Confirm would be up and running by July 1992. AMRIS also promised to limit the cost per reservation to $1.05.

It took AMRIS a year to finish the design phase, not seven months. At the end of that year, it made some revisions in the contract: the cost of the project would be $72.6 million, not $55.7 million; the cost per reservation would be $1.30 in the first year of operation, not $1.05; and the timetable for finishing Confirm would have to be extended by one month. Each partner was given an opportunity to withdraw from the project at this point, but none did.

In February 1991, AMRIS presented another revision to the development plan and price tag. According to the revision, only Hilton would be able to use the Confirm system by July 1992, the original completion date. The new price tag was now $92 million, not $72.6 million. By that summer, half of the employees working on the Confirm project were looking for new jobs. They were dissatisfied with managers who kept insisting on unrealistic schedules even though it was obvious that the project was in some trouble.

In April 1992, Hilton became the system's first beta-test user, and major technical problems surfaced. The chairman of AMRIS then wrote a letter to the other partners, confessing that the project had not gone according to plan. He admitted that the managerial team was inept and had concealed important technical and performance problems. He also admitted that the technical staff had failed to construct the appropriate interfaces and database for the multi-industry system. He concluded that Confirm was still fifteen to eighteen months from completion.[13]

In July 1992, the projected completion date, the Confirm project was killed because technical difficulties could not be surmounted. The final amount that had been spent on this misadventure: $125 million. Lawsuits were filed and settled out of court in January 1994.

The Confirm story is instructive in at least two ways. First, it can help us appreciate how difficult it is to antici- pate the outcome of an information system design project. Actually, the only thing unusual about the Confirm story is the amount of money lost; these kinds of failures are very common in the software development field. Consequently, information specialists need to be especially cautious when making promises about when a new product or service will be operational. Often, the natural human tendency is to minimize problems and overestimate one's abilities to get the job done. It is best to play it somewhat conservative and allow for unforeseen delays and glitches.

A good antidote to the temptation to make unrealistic promises is to provide for flexibility in the planning pro- cess. Develop best-case and less-than-best-case scenarios from the outset and educate your customers about the po- tential for delays due to unforeseen problems. Refer to in- dustry standards and professional association guidelines whenever possible in this cautionary planning. Establish good communication habits with all stakeholders from the outset and be quick to tell them about delays and difficul- ties. Promising to do your best to achieve an agreed-upon goal is more honest than making a promise to meet the goal no matter what. The principle of fair representation ought to remind us to be realistic in this way. Managers who only want to hear and see the good news, like the managers on the Confirm project, are putting themselves in an unneces- sarily precarious moral position.

Second, the Confirm story can also help us to appreciate

the moral significance of good communication practices within an organization. Honesty is imperative when dealing with customers and business partners; it is perhaps even more imperative when dealing with employees. A key managerial virtue that is often overlooked, I believe, is humility. Humility has the same root as *humus,* which is the Latin term for dirt. Like dirt, or the earth, the humble person is able to accept whatever gets dumped or discarded and turn it into something new and fresh. We usually think of honesty as pertaining to what *we* say and do. But there is also a kind of honesty that pertains to what we can hear and see in others: that's what I mean by humility. The humble manager is able to absorb the concerns and worries of his or her employees and respond creatively to them. The humble manager does not ignore bad news, as the Confirm managers apparently did; on the contrary, nobody is more willing to hear the truth on its own terms, whatever they may be. For that reason, nobody is better able to respond positively to circumstances as they unfold than the humble manager either. This is another aspect of the moral life that the principle of fair representation should call to mind.

In sum, it is better to play it conservative than to get into the bad habit of overestimating what you or your company can accomplish. A new term—*vaporware*—has been invented to depict nonexistent information technology products that were announced too soon. It might be easier to conceive new products and start-up ventures in the computer age, but it is also probably more difficult to bring them into reality.

Even more difficult than bringing a new information technology product into commercial being is keeping it there. Competition is cutthroat and fierce. The playing field can change overnight, as the appearance and sudden ubiquity of the World Wide Web demonstrates. Richard Spinello has argued that high-tech vendors have a moral responsibility to make plans for the ongoing support of their products when and if they encounter setbacks such as bankruptcy. Vendors must provide adequate *prospective* information to customers given the uncertainties of the information technology industry. Spinello suggests that conscientious companies take four steps to ensure the ongoing usefulness of their products:

1. Companies should place the source code for software products in an escrow account with instructions that it be made available to customers if product support is totally discontinued because of bankruptcy. With the source code in hand, some customers will be able to fix bugs, upgrade their systems to match new hardware, and so forth.
2. Companies should be candid about their future prospects with potential customers so that they can make better purchasing decisions. It would help prospective customers of private companies, in particular, to know how they are set financially.
3. In the event of a takeover or merger, companies should make ongoing product support a major negotiation issue. They should zealously protect the rights of their customers.
4. Companies should make efforts to provide at least a one-year notice if it becomes necessary to discontinue product support. Most contracts only stipulate a thirty-

day notice, which is probably inadequate given the expense and complexity of information technologies and the vulnerability of customers who rely heavily on vendor-provided technical support.[14]

Summary

Business transactions are grounded in moral trust and promise keeping; without a moral framework, in fact, commerce as we know it would not be possible. Many laws have been passed to help buttress the morality that supports business culture. Ironically, we sometimes forget that the law is designed to serve morality and not replace it completely. The ethical principle of fair representation can help us to emphasize the importance of morality in good business, which may then bring us some relief from the penchant for litigation in America. Simply by treating people with moral fairness, we can take away some of the reasons for resorting to the law. Fair representation must also make us aware of unique high-tech moral issues such as vaporware, and it must educate us about the vulnerabilities of customers who invest major resources and trust in information technology products.

The same problems that we saw in chapter 2 regarding intellectual property law are relevant to the discussion of liability law in this chapter. First, software defies prior legal categories in both instances: the machine versus text controversy in intellectual property law is analogous to the product versus service controversy in liability law. Second, a gap separating commonsense morality from the complexities of law is manifest in both instances. Whereas ethics mediated the gap with respect to intellectual property, it must play a recovering role with respect to liability. The principle of fair representation can help us to recover the moral import of liability law, thereby relieving the law of some of its responsibilities. Treating people with moral respect can actually improve business, as the story of Kingston Technology Corporation demonstrates. There are three categories of accountability in product liability law: strict liability without fault, warranties and disclaimers, and negligence. Except in the case of strict liability, more attention to morality would probably lessen the need for litigation.

Intel did not manage its flawed Pentium chip problem with appropriate moral vigor. The company did not acknowledge the flaw as soon as it was confirmed; nor did it stop shipping flawed chips immediately; nor, finally, did it move fast enough to assure customers that it would do everything possible to fix the problem. Once honesty is compromised even slightly, as in the Pentium case, it snowballs into an avalanche because virtues such as honesty represent a delicate balancing act between competing vices. Lose your balance, and you fall hard: that is a fact of morality as well as physics. Although honesty about bugs is imperative, it is not sufficient; companies such as Intel must also take quick action to correct mistakes. The principle of fair representation can boost our sense of moral service on behalf of the customer; it should also encourage companies to adopt whistle-blowing policies that allow employees to express moral concerns in a confidential setting.

American Airlines and its partners got stung for $125 million in a failed attempt to market its reservation system expertise to other travel-related areas of business. The Confirm story indicates how difficult it is to finish an information system design project and consequently the need to be cautious when estimating what can be done. The principle of fair representation should remind us to be realistic in our planning and flexible in our promises. The Confirm story also indicates the need for humble management. The humble manager is capable of seeing and hearing the truth more clearly, which is especially helpful in dealing with employee concerns. It isn't hard to conceive new products and start-up ventures in the information age, but it is hard to make them real, and harder still to keep them in the marketplace. Companies, therefore, have a moral responsibility to make plans for ongoing customer support in the event that they go out of business. Four steps are recommended: place the source code for software products in an escrow account; provide potential customers with adequate prospective information; negotiate vigorously on behalf of customers in the event of a takeover; and provide at least a one-year notice before discontinuing product support.

For Further Thought

1. Albert Carr wrote an article of some importance about the ethical use of bluffing in business.[15] He compares the competitive world of business to a poker game, arguing that it is acceptable to bluff in both instances because other "players" expect it. Do you think Carr is accurate in his interpretation—that is, do we really expect to be bluffed by the companies with

which we do business? How would you either counter or defend such an argument on moral grounds?

2. Microsoft's ballyhooed Windows 95 upgrade was delayed several times before final delivery to retail outlets in August 1995. There are two ways to look at this situation. Some would say that Microsoft engaged in a subtle form of vaporware by preannouncing its product before it was actually ready to be delivered, then, at the last minute, announcing a short delay. The psychological advantage of this strategy is that it creates a heightened state of anticipation in the marketplace. The business advantage of this strategy is that it freezes the software market to some extent. If you know that a new Windows platform is imminently forthcoming, you might hold off on buying new application software that was designed for the "old" Windows. The sooner the company convinces potential customers that a new platform is on the way, the sooner it will get the "wait and see" benefit of cautious buyers.

On the other hand, some would say that Microsoft's delaying actions were praiseworthy attempts to fix every bug before releasing its new product. Here, the delays can be seen as moral attempts to refrain from releasing inadequately tested software, which is the other side of the vaporware problem. Not only can information products be released too late (vaporware), they can also be released too soon.

It could be that the Windows 95 delays were the result of mixed motives (some vaporware, some fixing). How might we determine whether Microsoft was really promoting vaporware? What, if anything, would you do to prevent such practices?

Notes

1. Austen, *Pride and Prejudice,* 51–61.
2. Gladden, "Stop the Lifecycle, I Want to Get Off," 35–39.
3. "Doing the Right Thing," 64.
4. Prince, "Negligence," 848–55.
5. Quoted from a "Microsoft License Agreement" envelope, 1990.
6. Mason, Mason, and Culnan, *Ethics of Information Management,* 18–20; Price, "Pentium FDIV Flaw," 88 ff.
7. Kirkpatrick, "Fallout from Intel's Pentium Bug," 15.
8. Miller, "Once Lost, Can Trust Be Regained?" 79.
9. *Glengarry Glen Ross,* directed by James Foley (Rank/Zuprick Enterprises, 1992).
10. Miller, "Once Lost, Can Trust Be Regained?" 79.
11. DeTar, "Intel Alters Flaw Disclosure Policy," 32.
12. Oz, "When Professional Standards Are Lax," 29; Weinberg, "Budget Won't Budge," 20; Halper, "AMR Calls Confirm Partners Selfish," 4 ff.
13. Oz, "When Professional Standards Are Lax," 32.
14. Spinello, *Ethical Aspects of Information Technology,* 77–79.
15. Carr, "Is Business Bluffing Ethical?" 143–46. I learned of this article from Spinello, *Ethical Aspects of Information Technology,* 82–83.

Chapter 5

Nonmaleficence

Perhaps the most sensational news reports of the information age are "hacker" tales. Legendary hacker and fugitive Kevin Mitnick's arrest at an apartment complex in Raleigh, North Carolina, in 1995 illustrates the point. Apparently, Mitnick finally met his match when he broke into the home computer of Tsutomu Shimomura on Christmas Day 1994. Shimomura, a computer security expert at the San Diego Supercomputer Center, was so incensed about the break-in that he canceled a holiday ski trip and tracked Mitnick down from traces that he left on the Internet.[1]

Other hacker tales have been similarly enticing to the American public. For example, when hacker legend Kevin Lee Poulson was released from a five-year prison term for computer fraud in 1996, it was widely reported as a human-interest story. One of the stipulations of Poulson's probation was that he could not touch a computer for three years.

That is harder than it might seem, given the fact that you can't drive a car without indirectly using computer chips to regulate the fuel-injection system, among other things. Not wanting to take chances, Poulson dutifully checks with his probation officer first before using automated teller machines (ATMs), library catalogs, or any of the other computer devices that are now part of everyday life.[2]

Originally, hackers viewed themselves as civil servants of the high-tech frontier, perhaps comparable to the Doc Holiday types of the Wild West who broke the law plenty but also brought a certain brand of gun barrel justice to the new territories. We shall investigate the moral issues that pertain to hacking in this chapter about the principle of nonmaleficence, which means "doing no harm."

Nonmaleficence is one of the most venerable and ancient ethical principles of Western civilization. It sums up our commitment to care about the well-being of others. At minimum, according to this principle, we must never do anything that might contribute to the decline of another person's life or affairs. In chapter 1, I mentioned the reluctance that Karen Quinlan's doctors felt about disconnecting her respirator. Their reluctance was based on a commitment to do no harm. By disconnecting the respirator, they believed that Quinlan's well-being would be unacceptably diminished because her life would most likely end.

Computer crimes such as the fraudulent transfer of electronic funds from one account to another are so abstracted from ordinary life and its consequences that good people are occasionally lulled into believing it's OK to do that. It reminds me of negative numbers, which I first learned about in high school algebra. I never felt comfortable with them because they didn't seem real enough to me (−2 plus −2 equals −4, to be sure, but who has ever encountered −4 apples, oranges, or anything else?); computer funds suffer from the same "unreality" stigma, I believe. That is why it is especially important to keep the principle of nonmaleficence in mind. As everyday life becomes more complex and abstract, we need more reminders about what is good and what isn't.

Experts know that the typical computer criminal is not an ingenious hacker but a loyal employee who was probably overcome by temptation and opportunity.[3] It is crucial that we begin to appreciate how new technologies can affect our sense of moral balance. The information age is fraught with new temptations and new levels of temptation with which people didn't deal as often previously. Money or information that exists only in a computer file that only I know how to manage will work on my imagination. Overly tired one day, perhaps resentful toward the boss about some misunderstanding, it could happen that my better judgment will be overcome by the opportunity to steal electronically. Afterward, my conscience could be pacified to some extent because manipulating numbers on a computer is not the same thing as stealing a poor old lady's purse on the street—or so I would tell myself. This kind of moral lapse is happening to good people in the information age. We should be aware of it, and we should fight against the increased level of temptation by adopting ethical principles and perhaps instituting procedures that safeguard our morality in the workplace.

In addition to the hacker and crime issues, this chapter also focuses on the problem of fair competition. In American society, we are obligated to treat our business competitors fairly. This obligation has two sources: first, it is a matter of our common moral heritage that people should be granted fair opportunities to succeed in life; and second, it is a law of capitalist economics that competition is a necessary requirement for a healthy free-market system. Federal antitrust laws that prohibit monopolies are designed to ensure fairness for the sake of the economy and the consumer. The principle of nonmaleficence ought to remind us about the moral obligation to be fair because, quite simply, that is what being good requires.

It is extremely difficult to engage in hardball competition and yet maintain respect for the rules and boundaries of fair play that restrict competition. When you add expensive new information technologies to the equation, the balancing act becomes even more difficult because high-tech systems often change the way an industry conducts business. Company A may invent a new automation system that quickly establishes a new standard, which then forces companies B and C either to quit doing business or to pay company A for the use of its new system. Needless to say, the leverage that company A would hold over its competitors in this situation is incredible. What does fairness require? That is what we shall investigate. As one ethicist put it, information technologies ought to be used as a competitive tool but not a lethal weapon.[4]

Morality, Ethics, and the Law

In each previous chapter that was devoted to a specific principle, we wrestled with the often confusing relations between morality and the law. Regarding intellectual property, we saw how there is a growing gap between commonsense morality and the evolving complexities of copyright law in particular. It was suggested that ethics could mediate this gap between morality and the law. Adopting the ethical principle of respect for intellectual property enables us to (1) appreciate the competing purposes of the law (to reward innovators and to enhance the well-being of society as a whole), and (2) adjust our moral expectations to fit what the law requires in a complex information society.

Regarding privacy protection, we saw how the law is developing in a piecemeal fashion that often leads to confusion and inconsistency. In order to make up for the lack of comprehensive legal protection, it was suggested that ethics could encourage morality to take the initiative regarding privacy concerns. The ethical principle of respect for privacy reminds us to speak up on behalf of ourselves as self-determining individuals.

Regarding product liability, we saw how the law has become so all-encompassing that morality often gets overlooked despite the fact that the purpose of liability law is to ensure a moral framework for commercial exchanges. It was suggested that ethics play a recovering role to enhance the status of morality in buyer–seller relations. The ethical principle of fair representation reminds us that treating customers with moral decency will go a long way toward reducing the expensive habit of going to law in order to resolve civil problems.

Now, finally, we come to the problem of understanding how morality pertains to criminal law in the information

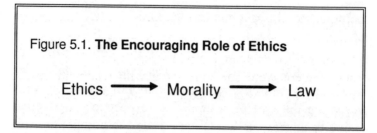

Figure 5.1. **The Encouraging Role of Ethics**

Ethics ⟶ Morality ⟶ Law

age as well as antitrust law. Laws to combat computer crime are being written in the same piecemeal fashion that we saw with privacy protection. There is no prior legal tradition that extends back to the Middle Ages, as with intellectual property, since computers are (obviously) a new electronic phenomenon. The Computer Fraud and Abuse Act of 1986 is comparable to the Privacy Act of 1974 in many respects. For example, both laws are fairly comprehensive in dealing with issues that pertain to government computers and information, but they don't address fraud and privacy in all the other sectors of society.

The encouraging role of ethics illustrated in Figure 5.1 indicates how we might improve our morality as it pertains to computer crime and hacking. Specifically, the principle of nonmaleficence must encourage us to be vigilant about the increasing number of temptations to crime that an automated society fosters. Every clerk and manager who understands the company's computer system is given a key to the squire's henhouse, in effect, with ample opportunities to pilfer an egg or a chicken once in a while. We need to speak up on behalf of conscience and not expect that it can always handle the increased load of saying no to immoral and criminal impulses. It often goes unreported because we don't have access to the human heart, but probably most people who engage in immoral and criminal behavior do so with mixed motives. They had alternative, better impulses that were temporarily silenced. How many good people could be helped in their internal struggles to do right or wrong if there were someone there with whom to talk? Companies might want to designate an ethics counselor who would be available for confidential discussions about matters of conscience.

I believe that we have a better chance of stopping high-tech crime by treating it as a moral problem rather than a strictly legal problem. More laws will not help the consciences of good employees to cope with more and more opportunities to do wrong. Instead, we ought to boost morality through policies and procedures that minimize employee isolation, which can lead to unbearable temptations. Ethics, in this case, ought to be teaching us to appreciate the fragility of our moral sensibilities and their need for nurture.[5] If more laws become necessary in order to provide a comprehensive net of protection against computer fraud and hacking, they should at least be attuned to the moral needs of average good people. The law should be in service to our morality and, if possible, take its lead from moral counsel, as Figure 5.1 suggests.

High-tech antitrust law is different than the criminal law represented by the Computer Fraud and Abuse Act. For one thing, it tends to be a function of presidential policy and politics.[6] The Federal Trade Commission (FTC) and the Department of Justice (DOJ) are the primary advocates of antitrust regulation. Regarding information technologies, these agencies focus primarily on two issues: tying arrangements and monopolization.[7] A tying arrangement involves the sale of one product on the condition that another product also be purchased. Tie-ins are unlawful when the seller has a dominant market position or interstate commerce is appreciably affected. IBM was prosecuted by the U.S. government for this kind of antitrust practice when it required purchasers of its tabulating-card machines also to purchase IBM tabulating cards.

Unlawful monopolization is slightly different and has two requirements for prosecution. First, the company under investigation must clearly possess monopoly power for a specific market. One of the biggest difficulties is how to define the market when information technology industries are so volatile and subject to change. Second, it requires clear evidence that the company under investigation acquired its monopoly power through willful, predatory conduct rather than by chance or superior manufacturing.

Microsoft Corporation, the largest software company in the world, has been under almost constant antitrust investigation in recent years. Governmental concern is understandable when you consider Microsoft's worldwide market share dominance:

- 82 percent of the PC operating system market;
- 64 percent of the Windows PC word-processing market;
- 61 percent of the Windows PC spreadsheet market;
- 60 percent of the Macintosh word-processing market;
- 89 percent of the Macintosh spreadsheet market.[8]

A number of predatory behavior charges have been lodged against Microsoft. One of them is that Microsoft unfairly requires computer makers to buy a copy of the Windows operating system for every PC they ship, whether the software is used or not. Another one is that Microsoft supplies its own application software programmers with better information about upcoming changes in its operating system than it supplies to competitor software developers. For the most part, Microsoft has avoided any major setbacks from antitrust litigation. The DOJ nixed a Microsoft deal to acquire Intuit, its major competitor and the market share leader for personal finance software. The DOJ also negotiated a consent decree or settlement with Microsoft about how it licensed its operating system to PC manufacturers, but it was struck down as too lenient and narrow in a review by Judge Stanley Sporkin. The judge has reopened the antitrust investigation against Microsoft and broadened it.

Many observers are skeptical about the value of antitrust judgments in such a volatile market as the computer industry. Changes come rapidly, and there is no clear evidence that competition is damaged by the presence of a major player such as Microsoft. For example, IBM successfully averted an antitrust breakup a generation ago when it dominated all aspects of the computer industry, hardware and software included. But look at IBM's position today: in the PC and software markets, it is a modest player. In the high-technology business, there is no predicting the future, except to say that constant innovation probably does an adequate job of ensuring fair competition.

Whether antitrust law is adequate to the task of safeguarding fair competition in American business is not a question we can answer here. What concerns us is the role

Figure 5.2. **The Recovering Role of Ethics**

Law ⟶ Ethics ⟶ Morality

that ethics and morality can play to enhance fair competition. I believe that ethics ought to play a recovering role in its mediation of antitrust law and morality. This is a different model than the encouraging role discussed above with respect to criminal law. We first encountered the recovering role in chapter 4 concerning fair representation.

As Figure 5.2 suggests, the principle of nonmaleficence ought to boost our morality in order to relieve some of the undue pressure Americans place on their legal system to solve every problem. If we demonstrate moral care for competitors, and also honor our cooperative business partnerships, then the FTC and DOJ will have less reason to police the marketplace. Every large corporation has a substantial legal department; perhaps a little moral counsel would actually save them some money.

Hacking and Computer Crime

In November 1993, the Hillsboro, Oregon, division of Intel Corporation filed criminal charges against Randal Schwartz for stealing a password and using it to gain access to its supercomputer division. Schwartz had been working at Intel as an independent consultant for five years before being arrested. Highly skilled in computer security,

Schwartz is perceived by many as a "godlike" hacker.[9]

In court, Schwartz told the jury that he was a computer nerd without many social skills. He had skipped two grades in school because of his talents and began working full-time with computers when he graduated at sixteen. Years later, Intel hired him as a security consultant for its supercomputer division. But Schwartz had disagreements with the staff and quit his contract early. Intel kept him on as a consultant for another division, however, and that is when the trouble started.

Without permission, Schwartz ran a password-decoding program called Crack on the computer system in his division. He obtained a valid password from the Crack test, which he then used to access the supercomputer division, where he formerly worked. He decided to run Crack on the supercomputer system because (1) he thought it would be fun to see how it worked on the fastest computers, and (2) he wanted to show the people for whom he used to work that their security had gone downhill since he left. Schwartz didn't try to hide these activities, and he used his own password, "Merlyn," to log in. Naturally, Intel authorities didn't see the "fun" in this activity and had Schwartz arrested.

Schwartz's story illustrates the clash of cultures that surrounds the hacker phenomenon. Computer hacking started in higher education, at MIT and Stanford, long before the advent of high-tech companies such as Intel. Gifted young people, some with limited social skills like Schwartz, were attracted to the new, exciting world of computing. There was a strong emphasis on sharing knowledge—software code, computer design, and so forth—which is part of the higher-education experience. Computing was a new science, and these young "hackers" were eager to dissect everything in order to learn how it worked. Money was not at stake in these early days; instead, it was a legend-building culture comparable to medieval knighthood, in which the hacker/knight displays exceptional skill for the sake of fun and glory.[10]

Commercialism changed everything. Secrecy and security replaced the openness of the universities when profit became the dominant motive rather than glory. In the economic culture that has taken over the computer world, the hacker mentality of open and free access to any computer system (with permission or not) is seen as criminal. We encountered this same commercial versus noncommercial culture clash previously in our discussion of intellectual property. It is one of the most important moral issues of the information age.

Recall from chapter 2 that the legal traditions for intellectual property protection have a dual, often contradictory purpose: to reward commercial invention and to help society as a whole to flourish. The problem is that the commercial side of the equation has been getting more attention than the societal side (not that the two goals need always be at odds), as a recent presidential white paper on intellectual property demonstrates. We must not forget that commercial interests aren't the only interests at stake. What's good for Intel isn't always necessarily good for the country.

I don't want to suggest that hackers like Schwartz are the good guys and corporations like Intel the bad guys. I only want to draw attention to the fact that commercial values aren't the only values that should have a voice here.

Schwartz attempted to defend his behavior by appealing to the hacker culture, which grew out of a different value system. His defense didn't work, and I don't believe it should have. If you willingly enter into a contract with a commercial enterprise, as Schwartz did, then you must honor that moral culture. The openly adventurous world of precommercial computing no longer exists, and the hacker spirit that grew out of that time must give way to the rule of law and its commitment to commercial values. But let's not overlook the noble qualities of hacking, which tend to be egalitarian like the education system that spawned it.

Nonmaleficence should remind us that hacking—i.e., entering a computer system without authorization—is both immoral and criminal. A hacker's curiosity about how something works—a noble virtue, certainly, in the right context—does not override the security concerns of computer owners. One person's freedom and curiosity end where another person's rights begin; that is a fact of life even in the most free and open societies. We cannot reduce all of our commitments to just one cultural value, even if it is the cherished American value of freedom, as hackers have tended to assume in their naïveté. We also have equally strong commitments to privacy and property ownership. Like it or not, hackers have to honor those commitments as well.

On the other hand, nonmaleficence should also remind us that it is harmful to society as a whole when commercial interests alone determine the laws of the land. Making money is important, but it isn't the only value we cherish; we would be just as naive as the hackers if we allowed corporations to convince us that their economic interests should always trump every other interest or moral concern.

Hacking has been criminalized in America because it entails a simplistic view of personal freedom that fails to account for the property rights of others. But hacking for fun or self-education should not be characterized in the same vein as computer sabotage, or computer fraud and theft, which are more serious criminal activities.

A new criminal vocabulary has evolved around the computer. Five terms in particular are noteworthy: *virus, worm, logic bomb, Trojan horse,* and *salami.* Viruses are self-replicating programs that may destroy files and crash systems by commandeering disk space. Typically, they pass from computer to computer through floppy disks. Worms are similar but more sophisticated. Like viruses, they are self-replicating programs that infect computers; but unlike viruses, they typically exist only in random-access memory (i.e., the "live" memory that is available for programming when the computer is turned on) rather than in disk storage. Typically, worms spread through networks. Logic bombs are programs that are triggered to begin once a period of time has passed or once a predetermined set of circumstances has occurred. Typically, a logic bomb, once triggered, will erase data files. Whereas viruses and worms may or may not be harmful to infected computers, there is no question that a logic bomb is designed to cause damage. Logic bombs are usually planted in a specifically targeted computer from the inside by a disgruntled employee; they don't infect computers randomly from the outside as viruses and worms do.

Viruses, worms, and logic bombs are examples of computer sabotage. The degree of criminality involved in sabotage cases depends on the intent of the criminal. In the Robert Morris case, which was mentioned in chapter 1, for example, the court was lenient because Morris did not intend to harm the Internet with his renegade worm program.

The Trojan horse and salami, on the other hand, are computer theft scams. The Trojan horse enables outsiders to penetrate the computer system of a bank or some other company that handles financial accounts electronically. This is reminiscent of the original "Trojan horse" ploy in Greek mythology. After years of fighting the Trojans to a standstill, Agammemnon, Odysseus, and the other Greek heroes determined that they must penetrate the high walls of Troy by stealth in order to win the war. They crafted a large wooden horse and rolled it up to the gates of Troy, then pretended to leave the battle in defeat. Overjoyed, the weary Trojans opened their gates and brought the horse into the city. They didn't realize that the belly of the horse was full of Greek warriors and that they had unwittingly let the enemy penetrate their seemingly infallible security system.

The computer version of the Trojan horse works the same way. It usually involves a planted program (the horse) that "innocently" queries the computer system in order to obtain legitimate log-in scripts and passwords. Then these legitimate paths into the system (the gates) are used to steal funds or valuable information.

In contrast to the Trojan horse, the salami is usually an insider's scam. Just as a good butcher can service many customers with one salami by cutting it into thin slices, a sly thief can make a large haul by reprogramming an accounting system to slice a few extra cents off of thousands of different electronic accounts and funnel the money elsewhere.

There is no question that computer crimes such as logic bombs and Trojan horse ploys are morally wrong. Theft is theft no matter what the means are for accomplishing it. Nevertheless, the principle of nonmaleficence can educate us about what high-tech criminals are up to so that we can blow the whistle when we see something suspicious happening. More important, nonmaleficence ought to remind us about who the high-tech criminals typically are—loyal employees with an opportunity. As I mentioned in a previous section, we need to understand the increased temptation to crime that is a consequence of high-tech automation. Moral conscience functions best when judging human-to-human interactions; the sense of isolation and abstraction from human interaction that occurs when we spend more time with computers therefore represents a moral challenge. Being aware of the challenge helps.

More specifically, job descriptions and workflow charts can be reviewed with an eye toward reducing employee isolation. We shouldn't burden individuals with unshared or unsupervised responsibilities when the stakes are high. Such isolation will eventually invite temptation, or suspicion if something goes wrong, which isn't fair to the employee. Remember what happened to Barings PLC, the 233-year-old London bank that was bankrupted in 1995 because the risky investments of Nicholas Leeson went sour. It turns out that the 28-year-old Leeson was both the trader and trade supervisor in the bank's Singapore office, meaning that he could hide his losses in the Tokyo stock and bond markets from senior managers . . . until it was too late. Leeson certainly bears most of the responsibility for his actions. But the bank is also blameworthy for placing Leeson in a position of moral isolation.[11]

A "buddy system" of checks and balances would help employees such as Leeson to interact with other people more, which is a necessary aspect of the moral life. We need to remind ourselves that morality is a human-centered experience. As we spend more time interacting with computers and less time with people, it makes sense that the moral resolve of at least some of us will suffer.

A sophisticated electronic auditing system might also prove helpful in reducing the increased moral temptation to commit crime by high-tech means. It could remove some of the opportunistic situations that, over time, work on the conscience and weaken its resolve.

Fair Competition

The rivalry between Ben Johnson of Canada and Carl Lewis of the United States in the 100-meter dash was the feature story of the 1988 Seoul Olympics. Everything about these two sprinters, it seemed, was a contrast in style: Johnson was short and muscle-bound, Lewis tall and graceful; Johnson had the quickest start from the blocks, Lewis the best finishing kick. It was a good rivalry that enhanced the image of track and field.

In the finals at Seoul, Johnson beat Lewis for the gold medal in world-record time. Afterward, however, Johnson failed a drug test for steroid use. The Olympic Committee decided to take back the gold medal and give it to Lewis instead. The use of performance-enhancing drugs is banned from athletic competition because they undermine its purpose, which is to test an athlete's *natural* abilities, grit, and preparedness. Drugs can alter the natural state to such an extent that an athlete could become better in competition without having had to work hard for it. Taking drugs to enhance one's natural talents is considered cheating; it is not conducive to fair competition.

Speed is the critical factor in sprint competition. Speed is to track and field what *access* is to an information society. Just as some athletes have tried to gain speed by cheating with high-tech drugs, some companies have tried to enhance their own access to information—or to limit the ability of their competitors to have equal access—by "cheating" with high-tech information systems. This sort of cheating is immoral (and potentially illegal, depending on circumstances) because it demonstrates a callous disregard for the two basic requirements of fair competition that are part of our cultural heritage.

First, fair competition requires a level playing field. Every competitor must be given an opportunity to win based solely on talent, luck, and effort. Likewise, every competitor must have a concern for the integrity of the game itself (whether the "game" involves athletics, business, school, or some other aspect of life). When Johnson took steroids, he skewed the playing field in his own favor; the incredible speed that he displayed in Seoul was not gained fairly. A comparable example regarding information technologies is the mid-1980s debate concerning airline reservation systems.

In 1985, approximately 70 percent of all computer reservations in the airline industry were handled on automation systems owned by just two carriers, United and American. That meant smaller carriers such as USAir were forced to pay a fee to the two bigger companies for 70 percent of their electronic bookings. Many of the smaller airlines joined forces to complain that the programming of the two reservation systems was skewed to favor the parent companies. For example, the cheapest fares and most convenient departures would not always appear on a travel agent's computer screen when they were offered by competitors of United or American. Early on, the Civil Aeronautics Board judged that such biased display programming was wrong.[12]

This example illustrates how complicated the notion of a "level playing field" can be in the information age. Clearly, companies such as United and American that expend their resources to develop sophisticated information systems deserve to profit from their considerable risks and efforts. But the reservation systems that United and American developed became so successful that they transformed how the airline industry works. Other companies could not *survive* without using the new systems. When the very survival of one's competitors becomes an issue, then a line has been crossed that extends beyond the realm of normal competition. *Fair* competition is how we designate that line: what enables competition to continue is considered fair, but what kills competition altogether (by means of "killing" one's competitors, in this instance) is unfair. This ability to transform an entire industry—to change the playing field, in other words—through technological innovation is something with which we must deal on a more frequent basis; nonmaleficence can be a reminder that we should not allow healthy competition to degenerate into a lethal business.

Second, fair competition requires a sense of care for the well-being of one's competitors. As one philosopher put it, being moral means that we never treat others as mere means to our own ends.[13] We must think of others—including corporations, if that is our context—as moral equals and honor them with equal treatment and consideration. Not only did Johnson skew the playing field in his own favor when he added to his speed by taking drugs, he also failed to care adequately for Lewis as a competitor. A comparable example regarding information technologies is the frequent complaint that Microsoft provides its own application programmers with better and more timely information about new features in its operating systems. If true, such practice is an unacceptable slight to Microsoft's competitors in the application software market who must also redevelop their products to fit new operating system features. Equal treatment as one aspect of fair competition would require Microsoft to share operating system information with all competitors in a timely manner.

Technology can't be blamed for the fact that cheating is part of human experience. But it does provide us with new opportunities for old tricks and habits, as we saw in the last section regarding the Trojan horse. That is why we need to boost our moral resolve by keeping in mind ethical principles such as the ones introduced in this book. No doubt it is often a fine line to draw between what is acceptable as fair competition in high-tech business and what isn't. The principle of nonmaleficence can help by reminding us of the two requirements for fair competition (level playing field, equal treatment) that were just discussed.

Summary

Sensational hacker tales have drawn attention to the potential for harm inherent to life in a computer-mediated society. One of the great moral dangers of our day is the temptation to think that stealing electronic data is not as serious as stealing the squire's chickens. The principle of nonmaleficence—doing no harm—is an ancient precept that sums up our commitment to care about the well-being of others. It can serve as an important reminder about what is right and wrong, and what is fair.

Laws to combat computer crime are being written in piecemeal fashion, which leaves it up to each one of us as individuals to formulate a comprehensive moral understanding of right and wrong computer use. The ethical principle of nonmaleficence can play an encouraging role in this regard, providing us with a brief reminder of our commitment to do no harm. On the other hand, antitrust laws to combat unfair competition are being saddled with perhaps too much of the burden to instill civility and fairness in business. The ethical principle of nonmaleficence can help play a recovering role in this arena, meaning that it should prompt us to take moral responsibility for how our competitors are treated.

Hacking, or the unauthorized use of computer systems, symbolizes the clash of commercial versus noncommercial cultures that we often encounter in the information age. Like scientists in university settings, hackers want to be free to pursue their curiosity about computers no matter where it leads; they tend not to respect the property rights that are crucial to commercial culture. The principle of nonmaleficence can educate us about the multiple commitments that we all must honor. More serious than hacking are computer sabotage crimes (viruses, worms, logic bombs) and theft scams (Trojan horse, salami). Nonmaleficence should also educate us about who high-tech criminals typically are—loyal employees with an opportunity. We ought to take measures to protect the moral vulnerability of employees by not burdening them with unsupervised responsibilities that might lead to temptation. Morality functions best in human-to-human interaction, not human-to-computer interaction.

Speed is to track and field what access is to information technologies; doping leads to unfair competition on the racetrack just as monopolization does in business. There are two basic moral requirements of fair competition in any arena. First, fair competition requires a level playing field; second, it requires a sense of care for one's competitors. The principle of nonmaleficence can help us to keep these requirements in mind as we try to live good lives in a competitive world.

For Further Thought

Much of the world's great literature over the past century has focused on problems associated with too much change. For instance, Franz Kafka's "The Metamorphosis" tells the story of Gregor Samsa, a World War I–era salesman in a large European city. Samsa was confronted with such a new, bewildering world— more and more heavy industry, round-the-clock facto-

---

ries, urban population explosion, loss of neighborhoods, fierce competition in every enterprise—that Kafka felt compelled to portray him as an insect. Confronting a human character in the guise of an incomprehensible cockroach, the reader is forced to experience some of the strangeness and fear that Samsa himself felt. Clearly, the message is that too much technologically driven change and competition is destructive and inhuman.

Yasunari Kawabata's *The Sound of the Mountain* tells a similar, though more subtle, tale about how the aftermath of World War II changed Japan and drove a wedge between parents and their children. Many changes after the war were technology-driven as Japan retooled itself for competition in Western-style industries.

There are signs that the postindustrial information society will also challenge our sense of place in the world. Information overload and computerphobia seem as threatening to human meaning as the overcrowded city with its dirty factories; and data-entry jobs are probably as demeaning and boring as their assembly-line predecessors.

Too much of anything can be harmful. That is a moral precept that goes back to the ancient Greeks, who gave us the idea that virtue entails striving for the mean (or balance) between two extremes. Happiness, for example, is the mean between sadness and giddiness; courage, the mean between fear and carelessness. The principle of nonmaleficence ought to remind us that too much technology and change can sometimes be harmful. As the Greeks would no doubt advise, we need to balance high-tech with what John Naisbitt calls "high touch."[14]

The more technology we have, the more we tend (and need) to interact with other people. That is Naisbitt's observation and precept for the information age. Computers and networks don't isolate us; they give us more opportunities to interact with one another. But we must take the right approach and not overlook our human needs. How well do you think we are balancing our high-tech and high-touch needs in the information age? Is there too much emphasis on technology, too little, or just the right amount? List any high-touch human needs that you think we need to care more about.

Notes

1. Dill, "Authorities Nab 'World's Most Wanted' Computer Hacker," A12.
2. Morello, "Top Hacker Has Tough Time Hacking Life Minus Computer," A10.
3. Icove, Seger, and VonStorch, *Computer Crime,* 118.
4. Spinello, *Ethical Aspects of Information Technology,* 58.
5. Nussbaum, *Fragility of Goodness,* 1–21. Nussbaum is one of the few ethicists to emphasize how much our moral lives are in need of nurture.
6. Melamed, "Antitrust," 13–15.
7. O'Connor, "Emerging Antitrust Issues Affecting the Computer Industry," 821–26.
8. Kirkpatrick and Schlender, "The Valley vs. Microsoft," 86.
9. Danks, "Intel Consultant on Defense," B1.

10. Levy, *Hackers,* 26–30.
11. Dalglish and Wallace, "Breaking the Bank," 46–48.
12. Carter, "Different Air War," 120.
13. Kant, *Ethical Philosophy,* 30.
14. Naisbitt, *Megatrends,* 39–53.

Appendix

Case Studies

The cases presented in this appendix will give you an opportunity to pull everything together from your reading of the previous chapters and make them applicable to real-life circumstances. Recall that I introduced a four-step method for applying principled ethics in chapter 1. You might want to go back and glance over that section ("Simple Is As Simple Does") once again before tackling these cases. Tables 1.1 and 1.2, which list the four principles of information ethics and summarize the four-step method, respectively, are reproduced here for your convenient referral. Please read through the cases and answer the questions posed at the end of each one. When appropriate, please use the four-step method to guide you, and remember that the purpose of ethics is to help you become a better moral agent.

Table 1.1

The Principles of Information Ethics

1. Respect for intellectual property
2. Respect for privacy
3. Fair representation
4. Nonmaleficence (or "doing no harm")

Table 1.2

The Four-Step Method of Principled Ethics

1. Get the facts straight.
2. Identify the moral dilemma (inspect the facts in light of your moral feelings).
3. Evaluate the moral dilemma using the principles of information ethics to decide which side has the most ethical support.
4. Test your solution: will it stand up to public scrutiny?

Case 1: Commercial Terrorism or Simple Repossession?

In January 1989, Revlon Group, the cosmetics giant with annual sales of $3 billion, hired Logisticon to develop an inventory-control software program for two of its four national distribution centers. Logisticon is a relatively small Silicon Valley company with less than $20 million in annual revenues. The software development contract was for $1.2 million.[1]

On October 9, 1990, Revlon notified Logisticon of its intention to cancel the contract and withhold any further payments. At that time, only $450,000 had actually been paid to Logisticon. Revlon contended that the software was not working properly. Revlon did not stop using the software program, however, even though the company was refusing to make further payments.

In the dead of night on October 16, 1990, Logisticon engineers gained telephone access to the Revlon computers at the Phoenix, Arizona, and Edison, New Jersey, distribution centers where their inventory software was being used. Using Revlon's access codes, the engineers entered the necessary commands to shut down the operation of their software and also scramble Revlon's shipment and inventory schedules. A few hours later, Logisticon president Donald Gallagher sent Revlon a fax notifying it of this act of electronic "repossession."

The two Revlon distribution centers were thrown into chaos and forced to cease operations for three days. Approximately four hundred workers were sent home for that period of time. Nationally, Revlon's shipments to the Northeast and West were temporarily affected. But Revlon's other two distribution centers in Jacksonville, Florida, and Oxford, North Carolina, were still functional.

Revlon spokesman James Conroy called Logisticon's midnight actions a form of "commercial terrorism." On October 22, 1990, Revlon filed a breach-of-contract lawsuit in San Jose, California. Among the disputed claims was that Logisticon contaminated and destroyed Revlon's database when it disabled the inventory software. The suit was settled out of court in January 1991; terms were undisclosed.

Using the method of principled ethics, please identify the moral dilemma in this case. In your opinion, which company has the moral edge, Revlon or Logisticon? Clearly, there is some fault on both sides, but which company is less at fault than the other one? That is, which company has more principles in support of its side of the dispute? That will determine which one has the moral edge.

Also, please take a moment to reflect on the metaphors that the two companies employed to characterize what happened. According to Revlon, Logisticon's actions were a form of *terrorism*. Does that characterization seem apt or justified? According to Logisticon, on the other hand, its actions were nothing more than a high-tech form of *repossession;* in other words, it did what a bank would do to recoup losses for delinquent car payments. Is the analogy to car repossession a good analogy in this instance? Finally, can you think of a better metaphor for what happened than the two provided by these companies?

Case 2: Fishy Business (Hypothetical)

John Flora is a lifelong resident of Beaverton, Oregon, who has fished practically every stream and pond in the Northwest. Fishing is his passion. After finishing his twentieth year of work as an engineer at Tektronics, John decided to start his own fishing business. He called his company Northwest CatchIt.

There are many good fishing guide and manufacturing companies in the Northwest, but none had specialized in serving the needs of the disabled. That was the niche market that John targeted for Northwest CatchIt. John's brother Mitch suffered from multiple sclerosis, which left him bound to a wheelchair. But Mitch still loved to fish and often accompanied John on his excursions to the backwoods. In fact, John had already invented several devices to make it more convenient for Mitch to go fishing with him. One of them was a special handheld wheelchair winch that John thought he could manufacture and sell.

In its first two years, Northwest CatchIt did fair business—enough to pay expenses and cover payments on a loan for handicapped accessible vehicles and equipment that had to be purchased. John advertised his company in magazines and newsletters that served the Northwest disabled community, and he dropped off brochures at local agencies and meeting places that the disabled frequented. But that wasn't generating enough inquiries to allow the business to grow and flourish. So John sought the advice of a marketing consultant.

The marketing consultant recommended two things, chiefly. First, she recommended that John broaden the scope of his advertising to include a national audience. There is every reason to expect that a disabled person in Iowa or Texas would enjoy a fishing trip to Oregon if given the right support and services. Second, she recommended that John do a direct-marketing campaign to a targeted audience. She provided the name of a large prosthetics company that would sell John a database with the names and addresses of its customers. He could begin his direct-marketing mailing with that list and see whether it made a difference.

John contacted Prosthesis and arranged to buy its database. He mailed a special three-day-weekend trip offer to the people listed in the database. Within a few days, telephone inquiries about the special began to come in. Business was picking up to the levels for which John had planned.

Then, John got a letter from a lawyer who represented one of Prosthesis's clients. It turns out that one person who was listed on the database John purchased was a three-year-old girl with a congenital hip problem. Understandably, her parents didn't like the fact that John's company was soliciting business from their three-year-old, and they wanted it stopped.

Please use the method of principled ethics to assess the moral issue at stake in this case. Which two principles are in conflict here? Does one side or the other have a clear moral edge? How would you resolve the conflict? What could database owners such as Prosthesis do to prevent this kind of problem from occurring in the future?

Case 3: The Browser That Would Be an Operating System

Netscape Communications is an upstart $3 billion company that is synonymous with the Internet—more specifically, the World Wide Web—in the minds of some people. The killer application that vaulted Netscape into the multibillion-dollar stratosphere is Navigator, a software program that allows users to browse the Web. Navigator thus far has been the dominant browser on the "market" (with an estimated 80 percent share in late 1996). "Market" is put in quotation marks here because of a peculiar quirk in browser competition: the main competitors, Netscape and Microsoft, have so far been giving their products away for free.[2]

Microsoft Corporation is a $70 billion company that is synonymous with PC software, particularly operating systems. The killer applications that have sustained Microsoft as the most successful software company in the world are DOS and Windows. Microsoft is also famous for its come-from-behind successes in key competitive markets. For example, Microsoft's word-processing application software—Word—eventually displaced the original market leader, WordPerfect, because the company Bill Gates built has uncanny tenacity and marketing skill.

Lately, the competitor that Microsoft has focused as much as $2 billion per year in research and development to overtake is Netscape. That is serious money, at least six times the annual revenues of Netscape. Not only that, Microsoft is flooding the Internet with free Internet-related software, chiefly its own Web browser, Explorer 3.0. Released in August 1996, Explorer 3.0 notched 1 million downloads in its first week of availability. Why is Microsoft so worried about Netscape, a company not one-twentieth its size?

More is at stake than just the browser market. If Netscape has its way, Navigator will become the equivalent of a new-generation operating system that uses the whole Internet as its desktop. Coupled with applications written in Sun Microsystem's Java script, Navigator could conceivably make Windows obsolete. Local files, networked application programs, and distant Web pages alike could be managed with the same Navigator software, leaving virtually nothing for Windows to do. In fact, if browser-based Internet computing becomes the norm, then the PC itself could also become obsolete. Netscape recently released information about a new venture company called Navio, which will attempt to put browser software on a whole host of electronic appliances, including televisions, video games, and cellular phones. Microsoft's success to date has been tied to the success of the PC; if the PC goes, what happens to Microsoft? The stakes are indeed high in the battle over the browsers, which pits the dominant PC-based software company (Microsoft) against one of the new Internet-based software companies (Netscape).

Please refer to the principle of nonmaleficence to evaluate the relative moral positions of the two companies regarding software giveaways. Netscape is a start-up company that began giving its browser away for free in order to capture market share and make a name for itself. Marc Andreesen, Jim Clark's original partner at Netscape, is actually the person who invented the prototype Web browser—called Mosaic—as a student at the University of Illinois. Microsoft, on the other hand, is a fully established company that dominates the software industry in many markets. A latecomer to the browser market, Microsoft gives its software away for free in order to woo customers away from Netscape (keep in mind also that Navigator is a potential competitor for Windows). In your opinion, do both companies have equal moral standing with respect to their giveaways? Has the competition gone too far, crossing the line of what is fair? Do any other principles of information ethics support either Netscape or Microsoft in their giveaway strategies?

Case 4: The Zealous Hackers (Hypothetical)

Rental Security is a Chicago company that provides services and products in support of apartment-complex management companies. In the past, most of its revenue came from the sale and installation of security systems and the provision of nighttime security guard spot checks. Recently, however, there had been more frequent requests for background information about prospective renters. Specifically, apartment-complex managers now wanted to know whether rental applicants had any history of landlord disputes. Experience taught them that often their most troublesome clients—the ones with whom they wanted to avoid signing lease agreements—tend to be repeat offenders. A local media story about a man who lived practically rent-free for five years by conning one apartment manager after another also helped to instill the conviction that repeat offenders cause the most trouble.

In response to these more frequent requests for local background checks, Rental Security hired two software engineers to create a database for storing and retrieving information about bad renters. The database records were created from local sources such as police and court records, public notices, and rental association alerts, as well as credit reports from one of the national bureaus. Included in each record was the name of the person in question, last known address, employment history (if available), financial background, and a brief history of any landlord problems.

Initially, the goal was to use the database solely for background checks conducted by Rental Security. But then the company realized that it could make a substantial profit by selling access to its records to anybody with a legitimate business need.

For thirteen months, Alissa Jackson had been searching the North Chicago area for an apartment without any luck or, as it turns out, any understanding of what her difficulty really was. Alissa and her seventeen-year-old son had relocated to Chicago from the East and were temporarily staying with a relative. On several occasions, she had found an acceptable apartment, filled out the application, and made a deposit, only to be told a few days later that the apartment was no longer available. After the third time, Alissa was concerned enough to call the manager back and ask for some advice on how she might do better in the future. That is when she was told about Rental Security's database and the fact that her name was in the database as a person with a history of landlord problems. This was puzzling indeed to Alissa since she was new to the area and had never lived in an apartment before.

Alissa called Rental Security to inform it that it had mistaken her for somebody else. This was the first complaint the company had ever received about its new database, and although Alissa was treated courteously, there was confusion about what to do. In the meantime, Alissa was turned down by yet another apartment-complex manager. Naturally, she was frustrated and decided to consult an attorney.

Alissa's son, Roger, had made new friends at school when he joined the computer club. Roger told them about the problem his mom was having with Rental Security.

Roger and two of his friends decided that they could help by hacking into the database and changing Alissa Jackson's record so that she wouldn't be hassled anymore. They asked an older acquaintance to help them get a password from Rental Security, then accessed the system via modem late one night. The young hackers found Alissa's record but couldn't get the system to let them edit the record. They tried several standard hack ploys that were mentioned in a book that the computer club owned, with no success. Then, they tried a disrupting command that was supposed to imitate a virus and temporarily confuse the security program. It seemed to be working, but then something happened and the screen went blank.

The next day, the database operator at Rental Security noticed that the system wasn't working properly. The records were scrambled together and wouldn't display properly when called up. One of the software engineers was called, and she determined that the system had probably been sabotaged. The police were notified. An audit trail from the late-night modem connection eventually led police to the home of the computer club member whose computer had been used for the hack at Rental Security. The story soon broke in the media about three high school boys who just wanted to help a mom find a place to live. It was sensational news and sparked considerable discussion nationally about the need for accurate computer records.

Please consider the moral implications of this case. Do any ethical principles support the actions of the high school students? If so, which side in this dispute has the moral edge, the company or the hackers? Do you think this is a case in which the end (correcting bad data that was causing harm to an innocent citizen) justifies the means (hacking into the database to make changes that the company was slow to make itself)?

Notes

1. Richards, "Revlon Suit Revives the Issue of 'Sabotage' by Software Firms," C1; Siegman, "Computer Firm Shuts Down Revlon Giant," A1; Spinello, *Ethical Aspects of Information Technology,* 109–10.

2. Ramo, "Winner Take All," 56 ff.; Schlender, "Software Hardball," 107 ff.

Bibliography

Alderman, Ellen, and Caroline Kennedy. *The Right to Privacy.* New York: Knopf, 1995.

Aristotle. *Nicomachean Ethics.* Translated by Martin Ostwald. C. 330 B.C. Reprint, Indianapolis: Bobbs-Merrill, 1962.

Austen, Jane. *Pride and Prejudice.* 1813. Reprint, New York: Penguin Books, 1981.

Bellah, Robert, Richard Madsen, William Sullivan, Ann Swidler, and Steven Tipton. *Habits of the Heart: Individualism and Commitment in American Life.* Berkeley: University of California, 1985.

Betts, Mitch. "Dirty Rotten Scoundrels?" *Computerworld* 29 (May 22, 1995): 101 ff.

Beauchamp, Tom, and James Childress. *Principles of Biomedical Ethics.* 3d ed. New York: Oxford University Press, 1989.

Bjerklie, David. "E-mail: The Boss Is Watching." *Technology Review* 96 (April 1993): 14–15.

Blalock, Rick. "Don't Copy That Floppy." *Black Enterprise* 26 (October 1995): 46 ff.

Borgmann, Albert. *Crossing the Postmodern Divide.* Chicago: University of Chicago Press, 1992.

Bottoms, David. "Jim Clark: The Shooting Star @ Netscape." *Industry Week* 244 (December 18, 1995): 12–14 ff.

145

Branscomb, Anne Wells. *Who Owns Information?: From Privacy to Public Access.* New York: Basic Books, 1994.

Carr, Albert. "Is Business Bluffing Ethical?" *Harvard Business Review* (January–February 1968): 143–46.

Carter, Craig. "A Different Air War." *Fortune* 111 (February 18, 1985): 120.

Casarez, Nicole. "Electronic Mail and Employee Relations: Why Privacy Must Be Considered." *Public Relations Quarterly* 37 (summer 1992): 37–40.

Dalglish, Brenda, and Bruce Wallace. "Breaking the Bank." Macleans (March 13, 1995): 46–48.

Danks, Holly. "Intel Consultant on Defense." *Oregonian,* July 22, 1995, B1.

Darwin, Charles. *The Voyage of the Beagle.* 1839. Reprint, New York: Dutton, 1959.

David, Paul. "Intellectual Property Institutions and the Panda's Thumb: Patents, Copyrights, and Trade Secrets in Economic Theory and History." In *Global Dimensions of Intellectual Property Rights in Science and Technology,* edited by Mitchel Wallerstein, Mary Mogee, and Roberta Schoen, 19–61. Washington, DC: National Academy Press, 1993.

DeTar, Jim. "Intel Alters Flaw Disclosure Policy." *Electronic News* 41 (February 6, 1995): 32 ff.

Dill, Stephen. "Authorities Nab 'World's Most Wanted' Computer Hacker." *Oregonian,* February 17, 1995, A12.

"Doing the Right Thing." *Economist* 335 (May 20, 1995): 64.

Eder, Peter. "Privacy on Parade: Your Secrets for Sale!" *Futurist* 28 (July–August 1994): 38–42.

Edney, Leon. "Lament for a Shipmate." *Washington Post,* May 21, 1996, A19.

Forester, Tom, and Perry Morrison. *Computer Ethics: Cautionary Tales and Ethical Dilemmas in Computing.* Cambridge, MA: MIT Press, 1990.

Forrest Gump, directed by Robert Zemeckis. Paramount Pictures, 1994.

Gates, Bill. *The Road Ahead.* New York: Viking, 1995.

Gladden, G.R. "Stop the Lifecycle, I Want to Get Off." *Software Engineering Notes* 7, no. 2 (1982): 35–39.

Glengarry Glen Ross, directed by James Foley. Rank/Zuprick Enterprises, 1992.

Gogol, Nikolai. *Dead Souls.* Translated by David Magarshack. 1842. Reprint, New York: Penguin Books, 1961.

Greenberg, Ilan. "Getting Tough on IS Crime." *InfoWorld* 17 (May 1, 1995): 27 ff.

Halper, Mark. "AMR Calls Confirm Partners Selfish." *Computerworld* 27 (May 24, 1993): 4 ff.

Hauptman, Robert, and Susan Motin. "The Internet, Cyberethics, and Virtual Morality." *Online* 18 (March 1994): 8–10.

Howard, Philip. *The Death of Common Sense.* New York: Random House, 1994.

Icove, David, Karl Seger, and William VonStorch. *Computer Crime: A Crimefighter's Handbook.* Sebastopol, CA: O'Reilley and Associates, 1995.

Johnson, Deborah. *Computer Ethics.* 2d ed. Englewood Cliffs, NJ: Prentice Hall, 1994.

Jonas, Hans. *The Imperative of Responsibility: In Search of an Ethics for the Technological Age.* Chicago: University of Chicago Press, 1984.

Jurassic Park, directed by Steven Spielberg. Universal Pictures and Amblin Entertainment, 1994.

Kafka, Franz. *Selected Short Stories of Franz Kafka.* Translated by Willa Muir and Edwin Muir. New York: Modern Library, 1952.

Kallman, Ernest, and John Grillo. *Ethical Decision Making and Information Technology: An Introduction with Cases.* Watsonville, CA: McGraw-Hill, 1993.

Kant, Immanuel. *Ethical Philosophy.* Translated by James Ellington. 1785–97. Reprint, Indianapolis: Hackett Publishing, 1983.

Kawabata, Yasunari. *The Sound of the Mountain.* Translated by Edward Seidensticker. New York: Perigee Books, 1970.

Kidder, Rushworth. "Tough Choices: Why It's Getting Harder to Be Ethical." *Futurist* 29 (September–October 1995): 29–32.

Kirkpatrick, David. "The Fallout from Intel's Pentium Bug." *Fortune* 131 (January 16, 1995): 15.

Kirkpatrick, David, and Brenton Schlender. "The Valley vs. Microsoft." *Fortune* 131 (March 20, 1995): 84–86 ff.

Kohák, Erazim. *The Embers and the Stars: A Philosophical Inquiry into the Moral Sense of Nature.* Chicago: University of Chicago Press, 1984.

Levy, Steven. *Hackers: Heroes of the Computer Revolution.* New York: Doubleday, 1985.

Mason, Richard. "Applying Ethics to Information Technology Issues." *Communications of the ACM* 38 (December 1995): 55–59.

Mason, Richard, Florence Mason, and Mary Culnan. *Ethics of Information Management.* Thousand Oaks, CA: Sage, 1995.

Melamed, A. Douglas. "Antitrust: The New Regulation." *Antitrust* 10 (fall 1995): 13–15.

Mill, John Stuart. *Utilitarianism.* 1863. Reprint, Indianapolis: Hackett Publishing, 1979.

Miller, Arthur. *The Portable Arthur Miller.* Edited by Harold Clurman. New York: Penguin, 1971.

Miller, Michael. "Once Lost, Can Trust Be Regained?" *PC Magazine* (February 21, 1995): 79–80.

Morello, Carol. "Top Hacker Has Tough Time Hacking Life Minus Computer." *Oregonian,* September 22, 1996, A10.

Morrow, Lance. "Yin and Yang, Sleaze and Moralizing." *Time* (December 26, 1994): 158.

Naisbitt, John. *Megatrends: Ten New Directions Transforming Our Lives.* New York: Warner Books, 1982.

Negroponte, Nicholas. *Being Digital.* New York: Knopf, 1995.

Nussbaum, Martha. *The Fragility of Goodness: Luck and Ethics in Greek Tragedy and Philosophy.* New York: Cambridge University Press, 1986.

O'Connor, Kelly. "Emerging Antitrust Issues Affecting the Computer Industry." *Hastings Communications and Entertainment Law Journal* 17 (summer 1995): 819–39.

Oliver, Gordon. "Oregon Vehicle Owners Pop Up on Internet." *Oregonian,* August 7, 1996, A1 ff.

Orwell, George. *Nineteen Eighty-Four.* New York: Harcourt Brace, 1949.

Oz, Effy. *Ethics for the Information Age.* New York: Business and Education Technologies, 1994.

———. "When Professional Standards Are Lax: The Confirm Failure and Its Lessons." *Communications of the ACM* 37 (October 1994): 29–41.

Parker, Donn, Susan Swope, and Bruce Baker. *Ethical Conflicts in Information and Computer Science, Technology, and Business.* Wellesley, MA: QED Information Sciences, 1990.

Price, Dick. "Pentium FDIV Flaw—Lessons Learned." *IEEE Micro* 15 (April 1995): 88 ff.

Prince, Jim. "Negligence: Liability for Defective Software." *Oklahoma Law Review* 33 (1980): 848–55.

Ramo, Joshua. "Winner Take All." *Time* (September 16, 1996): 56 ff.

Rawls, John. *A Theory of Justice.* Cambridge, MA: Harvard University Press, 1971.

Richards, Evelyn. "Revlon Suit Revives the Issue of 'Sabotage' by Software Firms." *Washington Post,* October 27, 1990, C1.

Roszak, Theodore. *The Cult of Information: A Neo-Luddite Treatise on High Tech, Artificial Intelligence, and the True Art of Thinking.* Berkeley: University of California Press, 1994.

Samuelson, Pamela. "A Case Study on Computer Programs." *Global Dimensions of Intellectual Property Rights in Science and Technology,* edited by Mitchel Wallerstein, Mary Mogee, and Roberta Schoen, 284–318. Washington, DC: National Academy Press, 1993.

———. "Intellectual Property Rights and the Global Information Economy." *Communications of the ACM* 39 (January 1996): 23–31.

Schlender, Brent. "Software Hardball." *Fortune* 134 (September 30, 1996): 107 ff.

Seligman, Daniel. "The Devil in Direct Marketing." *Fortune* 123 (March 11, 1991): 123–24.

Siegman, Ken. "Computer Firm Shuts Down Revlon Giant." *San Francisco Chronicle,* October 25, 1990, A1.

Spinello, Richard. *Ethical Aspects of Information Technology.* Englewood Cliffs, NJ: Prentice Hall, 1995.

Stoll, Clifford. *Silicon Snake Oil: Second Thoughts on the Information Highway.* New York: Doubleday, 1995.

Tenner, Edward. *Why Things Bite Back: Technology and the Revenge of Unintended Consequences.* New York: Knopf, 1996.

Weinberg, Neil. "Budget Won't Budge." *Forbes* 153 (January 17, 1994): 20 ff.

Wiegner, Kathleen. "The Trouble with E-mail." *Working Woman* 17 (April 1992): 46.

Wolf, Gary. "The Curse of Xanadu." *Wired* (June 1995): 137 ff.

Index

Richard Severson earned his Ph.D. in theology and ethics from the University of Iowa, as well as a master's degree in library science. He has taught and worked as a librarian at several colleges and universities in Iowa and Oregon. Currently, he is Electronic Resources Librarian at Marylhurst College in Marylhurst, Oregon. Dr. Severson is the author of two prior books: *Time, Death, and Eternity* and *The Confessions of St. Augustine.*